Getting Afloat in a Sports...

Getting Afloat in a Sportsboat or RIB
is a Getting Afloat Publication.
www.gettingafloat.co.uk

Published by Thameside Publishing
PO Box 3, Goring-on-Thames,
Reading. RG8 0HQ
Tel: 01491 875703 Fax: 01491 872217
thamesidepublishing@goring.co.uk

Design by Louise Hillier Designs
e-mail: louise@hillierdesigns.co.uk
www.hillierdesigns.co.uk

Printed by The Lavenham Press
Lavenham, Suffolk. Tel: 01787 247436

© Thameside Publishing Ltd. 2012
ISBN   978-0-9570370-0-7

Contents...

Photographers include: Joe McCarthy, Tom Isitt, Peter Caplen, Emrhys Barrell

REGAL

Introducing the all new Regal 24 FasDeck, following the success of the 2220 this new boat has really steeped it up a gear, a new "Arena" seating layout gives even more space and a fantastic layout! The 24 FasDeck features a full sized head compartment and huge bow area that converts into a second sun pad! With all of these features the 24 FasDeck makes the perfect family sports boat.

Regal 24 Fasdeck

Regal 1900

The Regal 1900 is the sta... beautiful relationship with a... builder that can grow wi... throughout your boating caree... 1900 is everything you need! Sh... the looks, space and build o... couple these with the award w... "FasTrac" hull design and blis... performance adds to the list. S... fantastic all rounder and is also... trailerable, see for yourself, ar... your test ride...

Regal's 28 Express simply has it all, a great cockpit layout with lots of storage, the new electric folding radar arch complementing the full camper canvas and a huge cabin that will blow you away! The saloon is bright and has an excellent layout, a well equipped galley and the largest head in her class, marry this with a queen sized aft cabin and class winning head compartment and you needn't look at anything else!

Regal 28 Express

Gibbs Boat Sales are a premier Regal dealership with over 30 years of collective experience. Over time, Regal, a family owned independent manufacturer have invested heavily in R & D and every season roll out new models at the cutting edge of design. Gibbs Boat Sales staff have worked closely with Regal over these decades and have grown into one of the largest International Dealerships, we continue to provide customers with fantastic boats and excellent customer satisfaction. We look forward to seeing you soon.

Gibbs Boat Sales London

The Boathouse, Russell Road, Shepperton, TW17 9HY
TEL: 01932 242977

Gibbs Boat Sales Poole

The Waterfront, Cobbs Quay Marina, Hamworthy, Poole, BH15 4EL.
TEL: 07802 675011

www.gibbsboatsales.co.uk
sales@gibbsmarine.co.uk

GIBBS

Setting New Standard

Welcome Aboard

For many people their first boat is a sportsboat, sportscruiser, inflatable or RIB. And the reasons are obvious. They are the cheapest boats to buy and run, and they are the easiest to handle. They are versatile, meaning you can take them for a fast dash across the sea, or just go for a peaceful potter on the river or up the estuary. They will carry just the two of you, or the whole family. You can ski behind them, and you can sleep in them overnight.

If you keep your boat on a trailer at home you avoid the costs of mooring, and you can tow it to different waterways round the UK. And if you are really adventurous you can take it abroad. How about arriving in San Tropez or Monte Carlo in your own boat?

But you do need to make sure you have bought the right boat, and know how to use it safely. In this book we guide you through all the steps you need to take, chapter by chapter.

First Decisions helps you decide on the right boat for you, and where you want to use it. **Buying** takes you through all the steps, whether you are going for new or secondhand. **Engines** describes all the options for powering your boat. **Finance & Insurance** helps you raise the money, and then keep your investment protected.

Equipment and Electronics tell you the extras you need to buy and how to use them. **Training** is vital if you are to enjoy your boating and keep you and your family safe. And don't look on this as a chore – take all the crew along and it becomes a fun couple of days, as well as teaching you things that will serve you through the rest of your boating life. **Where to Go** gives you suggestions for your first trips, both at home and abroad.

Waterskiing & Wakeboarding tells you how you can safely tow the kids or adventurous adults behind your boat. **Racing** tells you where you can watch this exciting sport, or even take part in it yourself. And finally **Maintenance** gives you all the tips for keeping your boat and trailer in top condition and ready to go.

To find out any changes that may take place after this book is published, and keep up with the latest news and information, visit our **Getting Afloat** website, **www.gettingafloat.co.uk**

And remember - the boat you have the most fun in is the first one you ever own. So get yourself afloat.

See you on the water

Emrhys Barrell

Above:
This 22ft sportscruiser has a single petrol stern-drive, accommodation for two people, and will take you along the coast

Chapter 1:
First Decisions

So you have decided you want to get afloat in a sportsboat or RIB, but which one, and where?

The choices can appear bewildering, with conflicting advice from friends, salesmen, and self-appointed experts in the marina bar.

This Chapter will help unravel some of the mysteries, and outline the possibilities. It will arm you with the information you need to take to the boat shows or dealers, and get you on the water in the most appropriate boat for you and your family's needs, and your budget. We will cover where you should keep it, where you can use it, and what it will cost.

Top: This 19ft cuddy-cruiser has a single petrol inboard, and room for changing or overnight sleeping under the fore-deck. It will take you for sheltered coastal trips

Middle: This 20ft RIB will take you safely along the coast

Sportsboat or RIB?

The basic difference between these two boat types is their hulls. A sportsboat will have an all-rigid hull, usually made from glass reinforced plastic (GRP), but sometimes aluminium, or more rarely wood. A RIB on the other hand has a rigid underwater hull, but an inflatable tube round its gunwale, hence its full name - Rigid-bottomed Inflatable Boat.

A sportsboat will usually have more room inside, as the tube is not taking up the space. A RIB however will be able to tackle heavier seas, as the tube gives extra buoyancy heading into waves. Sizes of both go from 10ft to 33ft or more.

They can both be either entirely open or have cabins as we will describe below.

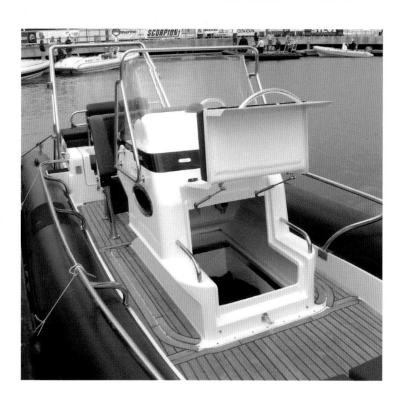

Bottom: This cabin RIB has room for a toilet under the console. Bigger versions offer seats or berths here

Cabin RIBs

A new development this, it takes the open plan of the RIB, but adds a cabin. Again this can be either a simple cuddy, giving space for changing or getting out of the rain, or a larger cabin with extra facilities. Sizes start from around 20ft.

Inflatables

These don't have the rigid bottom of the RIB, so can be rolled up into a bag, allowing you to carry them in the back of your car. They are more convenient to stow, but don't have the ability to tackle serious waves, so are usually only used in sheltered waters, in sizes up to around 12-15ft.

Personal Watercraft

The personal watercraft, or PWC, is also known as the jet-ski or wet-bike, which gives the clue to its style and use. It is a small craft, up to 12-14ft, that you sit on rather than in, in the style of a motorbike, and steer with handlebars rather than a wheel. They will usually only carry a maximum of two people, and are not for the faint-hearted. You can usually expect to get fairly wet on anything except the largest models, but they are exciting and fast. Also being small and light they are easy to tow and launch, making them ideal for single-handed boating.

Sportscruiser

This is a sportsboat with a cabin. This can be either just a simple cuddy, giving protection from the weather, and perhaps an occasional berth, or can be a cabin with full accommodation, including cooking facilities, a toilet, and perhaps a shower. Sizes usually start at 18ft or so.

This Page

Left: This 16ft semi-walkround boat has a practical layout, with plenty of room for half a dozen people

Opposite Page

Top: This cuddy-fisher also makes a practical family boat

Middle: The helm position of this RIB is designed for serious passages

Bottom: This personal watercraft gives exciting if wet fun

Which?
One for You

Let us now take a more detailed look at each type.

Sportsboats can come in several different layouts and styles. The original design had an enclosed bow, and a cockpit with either just two seats, side by side, or a second bench seat behind. These seats are low down, level with or below the gunwale. Steering is by a wheel set to one side, with a windscreen in front of you to keep off the wind and spray. Power is usually from an outboard, or sterndrive. An outboard takes up less space, being mounted on the transom. A sterndrive has its engine inside the boat, under a cover at the rear of the boat.

By the way, in case you are getting confused by some of the words we are using, you will find a list of the simplest boating terms at the end of this Chapter. We also describe dimensions in feet, but for a quick metric conversion, 10ft = 3m, 20ft = 6m, 30ft = 9m

The next development was the **bowrider**. This opens up the space ahead of the helm, making an extra seating area.

The advantages are more space in a given length of boat, and a more sociable seating arrangement. The downside is that this part of the boat bounces the most when you are traveling fast through waves. Also any large wave that might come over the bow will flood the boat. For this reason bow-riders are popular in the USA where you have many flat-calm lakes. Out at sea in the UK the forward area should only be used when the boat is moored, or at slow speeds, or in the calmest conditions, keeping an eye out for wakes from other boats. Also out at sea, the front area should be covered by a tonneau to keep the waves out. **Deckboats** have a squarer bow design, giving more seating or sunbathing space here.

The next sportsboat layout is the **walkround**. This has its helm position amidships, or towards the stern, with room to walk round it to get forward. The helm seating is usually quite high, giving a good view out over the water, and can either take one, two or three people. The rest of the passengers either sit along a bench behind the main helm seat, or ahead of the console, though with the same cautions about traveling

at speed as with the bow-rider. Walkrounds were developed from US sea-fishing boats, where the ability to play your catch as it swam round the boat was important. But it makes a versatile layout for general boating, with the option of a spot of mackerel fishing if you should wish.

The **dory** is a squarer, lower version of the walkround. It will often have what is know as a cathedral or trihedral underwater hull form, with three vee-shaped hulls running the length of the boat, rather that the one vee hull of most conventional boats. This makes it more stable at low speeds or at rest, but can give a harder ride at speed into head seas.

Cuddy cabins use the space under the fore-deck for limited overnight accommodation, with twin vee-berths, and sometimes a toilet under one of the berths. Headroom is limited to sitting only, though they can sometimes have a camper canopy over the cockpit, which you put up at night to give more space and headroom. You cannot use the cabin when the boat is underway, except at the slowest of speeds.

Sportscruisers extend the cabin principle, with more than half the boat length being given over to accommodation. Most will have a twin vee berth arrangement forward, with an infill converting this to a double. They will then have another double berth under the cockpit, but accessed from the cabin. In between will be a small galley on one side, and

Above: The French call them peche promenades, or fishing trip boats, but they still make practical family day-cruisers, with the larger versions having full accommodation forward

■ ■ ■ ▬▬▬▬

On The Water

The British Marine Federation's On the Water website, www.onthewater. co.uk has a mine of useful information about getting afloat, whichever activity you are interested in. They will also have stands and demonstration boat rides at several of the shows during the year

a toilet compartment opposite. Headroom in the main cabin will generally be just short of 6ft, while over the aft double it will be just 2ft or so. A camper canopy over the cockpit makes this into a living area, sometimes with the aft bench seat converting into another occasional berth. Thus you have enough accommodation for a family, and facilities for weekending or longer cruises.

Dayfishers are a design that has come over from France. Here they are called *peche promenades*, which loosely translates into fishing trips, though they are only occasionally used for angling. They will have a large aft cockpit, suitable for watersports, or the aforementioned fishing, plus a central upright wheelhouse. Depending on the length of the boat, this can just have seating for day trips, or a couple of berths, galley and toilet compartment. The deck layout will be in the walkround style. Again these are good multifunction craft, allowing you to put them to different uses.

The nearest British equivalent is the fishing cuddy boat. Again this majors on its aft cockpit, but the cuddy is right forward, with only sitting headroom.

All of the above designs can be powered by outboards or sterndrives. Outboard power is generally the norm up to 16-18ft, and stern-drives the norm

above 27ft, but in between you will find either. Big two-stroke outboards were very thirsty, so the four-stroke sterndrive was preferred, but the modern four-stroke outboard is as fuel efficient or more so than a stern-drive, with lower installation and maintenance costs, and has made major inroads in the 20-27ft range. Diesel sterndrives give better fuel economy.

Up to 25ft or so they will usually have single engines, but above this they can be twins, again either outboards or stern-drives. Two engines give greater security if you are travelling offshore.

RIBs came onto the scene in the 1960s and 70s. They were a development of the existing inflatables, with the flat canvas bottom being replaced by a deep-vee rigid GRP hull. This allowed them to drive into head seas at high speeds. The original RIB was developed by the lifeboat services, who were at that time using inflatables for inshore rescues. The flat-bottomed inflatable could not handle heavy seas at speed, but adding the rigid hull transformed the performance. They continued to be used by commercial operators and rescue services, but gradually their advantages for leisure use became apparent, to the point at which they are now a firmly established style of boat.

RIBs will generally be steered from a console, either

amidships or aft, with the seating either being benches, or jockey style. The latter keeps the occupants more firmly in place when the boat is bouncing through the waves, or turning fast. The layout was originally functional, mirroring the commercial ancestry, with plenty of grabrails to keep everyone in place, but gradually the styling has been softened, with more creature comforts.

Hulls will generally have a deeper vee section than a sportsboat, which combined with the buoyancy of the inflatable collar enables them keep up higher speeds in rougher head seas.

Today they have followed the evolutionary example of the 4x4 on the roads, with some models still being superb rough weather boats, but the majority giving performance and handling somewhere between a sportsboat and a rescue boat, whilst still maintaining the go-anywhere styling.

The logical development of this is the cabin RIB, where the addition of a cuddy has added some accommodation, to allow overnight or weekend cruising. These vestigial cabins are either part of the helm console, or under a separate foredeck, and can either have just a couple of berths, or more extensive facilities, including a galley and toilet. These boats generally start around 21ft.

Inflatables
Handy to carry, cheap to buy, an inflatable can make the ideal first boat. You will need a minimum 11ft (3.1m) to carry 2-3 people comfortably at any speed, with another foot or so giving more confidence. For safe planing you will need either an inflatable bottom, or a rigid slatted finish.

Hull design
At this point it is worth making a brief mention of hull design, and the effect it has on a boat's performance. Most of the craft you will be looking at will have a vee-shaped hull looking from behind. The angle of the vee bottom, relative to the horizontal is called the deadrise. The steeper the

Top: Shared ownership cuts your costs dramatically, and takes care of your boat's management – mooring, insurance and maintenance. It also allows you to own a larger craft than you could otherwise afford on your own, though prices will probably be £1,500 more than when this picture was taken

...angle, the better the hull is able to cut through oncoming waves, to give the occupants a smooth ride. However the flatter the angle, the less power is required to get the boat planing, ie skimming across the water.

Boats with a deadrise angle between 0-10 degrees are called shallow vee. Between 10-20 degrees they are called medium vee, and above 20 degrees deep vee. In fact in most designs the deadrise varies along the length of the boat, being deepest at the forward end, to cut through the waves, and shallowest aft at the transom, to give easy planing. However, as a generalisation, you will find deep vee hulls on boats used for racing, or for rough weather performance, medium vee hulls on general purpose sea-going craft, and shallow vees on lake boats.

Ski boats

A specialist design you will encounter is the competition ski-boat. It should be said that you can waterski or wakeboard behind just about any sportsboat or RIB, providing it has enough power, and either a ski-pole or ski-hooks on the transom, strong enough to take the strain of towing a skier, and in Chapter 9 we tell you how. But for professional competition skiing, around a set course on lakes, you need a specialist design.

This will be a boat with a carefully-designed, near flat-bottomed hull, to give minimum disturbance on the water behind, and to get swiftly onto the plane, aided by a huge inboard V8 petrol engine, with enough power, but more importantly enough torque, to pull a skier cleanly and quickly out of the water.

Because of their shallow-vee hull shape, these boats slam hard into waves, and are not generally used out at sea.

Left: This 20ft day-cruiser has twin berths and a portable toilet under the fore-deck, room for six people in the cockpit, and outboard power for economy

Where are you going to use your boat?

At this point you will have to decide how and where you are going to do your boating, and who with, as this will determine the type and size of craft you go for. The following suggestions are only generalisations - obviously as you get more experienced you may have different ideas as to the capabilities of yourself and your boat.

At its simplest, if you just want to take the family out on the river or lake in fine weather and calm conditions, then an inflatable up to 12ft, or a 13ft dory will be fine. The former you can carry rolled up in the boot, or on the roof of the car. The latter will require a simple, unbraked trailer, which you can tow behind any size car. Inflatables start around £1000-2000 including engine, with good secondhand examples from £750. A 13ft dory will be £8000 new, with a trailer £850.

If you want to go to sea, but again in sheltered areas, such as Poole Harbour, then you need to move up to a sportsboat or RIB, around 13-16ft (4-5m). A sportsboat will give more comfort, with bench or bucket seats, plus luxuries such as lockers and a stereo. A RIB will have more exposed seating, but will be better able to handle rougher conditions which can kick up even in sheltered waters. To tow this you may need a braked trailer, depending on the weight of the rig, and a medium-size saloon. Prices new start around £8000-12,000, with good secondhand examples from £5000. A trailer will be around £1400.

If you are wanting to go farther afield along our coasts, then you will need a boat 16-23ft (5-7m) long, either sportsboat or RIB. Towing this will require a large saloon, or smaller 4x4, especially if you

Below: Room for everyone. This 21ft (6.45m) RIB will carry eight people in sheltered waters, or five of you along the coast or across the Channel

Bottom: The dry-stack is the latest way of storing craft up to 30ft. As part of the fee your boat will be launched whenever you want it

Nautical terms

Earlier we promised to explain some of the nautical terms you will encounter, and here they are.

Bow
The front of the boat.

Stern
The back of the boat.

Amidships
Half way from front to back, or on the centreline.

Port
The left side of the boat, looking forward.

Starboard
The right side of the boat, looking forward.

Transom
The flat part of the stern.

Gunwale
The edge of the hull.

Keel
The lowest point of the hull.

Helm
The steering position. Also the steering wheel.

Rudder
The flat plate under water that steers the boat.

Outboards and sterndrives
Rotate to steer.

Galley
The cooking area. Never a kitchen on a boat.

Cockpit
Open seating area. Can be aft, forward or amidships.

Heads
What sailing boaters call the toilet. Motorboaters are happy to call it a toilet.

are going to be launching on steep or slippery slipways. New prices start around £15,0000 - £20,000, with secondhand fom £10,000. A trailer will be up to £2500.

If you want some limited accommodation, either for changing in, getting out of the weather, or overnight stops, then you will need either a cuddy cabin sportsboat, a cabin RIB, or one of the day-fishers. New prices start around £20,000 for cuddy sportsboats, £40,000 for a cabin RIB, and £21,000 For a day fisher. A trailer will be around £2500. Good secondhand examples start around 50% of the new price.

If you want to

take yourselves or the family on longer cruises, you will need a sportscruiser, 24ft (7.5m) and upwards. If you want to cross the Channel, we would advise at leat 24ft, preferably 27ft, and twin engines, in case one should break down. New prices start around £40,000 secondhand 50% of this.

Incidentally, even with a single-engine boat you can get extra security for longer trips by adding a small back-up outboard alongside the main one. This will get you to safety, albeit at a slower speed.

Where are you going to keep it?

The options for storing your boat are: at home, in a marina, or in a dry-stack. Each will have its pros and cons, especially regarding the cost. The simplest and cheapest option is to keep it at home on a trailer. No cost, but you have to tow it and launch it every time you use it, at £15-20 a time, plus the associated hassle.

The next step up is to keep it at home during the winter, but pay for a marina berth for the months of the summer you want to use it. Sounds good, but of course not every marina will have space for part-time moorings. As an alternative you may be able to store it on its trailer at the marina, and have them launch it when you need it. Some marinas are now offering this service, either with

your boat on its own trailer, or in purpose-built stacks, served by giant fork-lift trucks, which slide boats up to 30ft long in and out like slices of cake.

Charter a RIB

If you are not sure whether sportsboating is for you, how about getting a taste of what it is like for a day with an experienced skipper at the helm. UK Powerboat Charter will take up to ten of you on an adrenaline-packed trip round the Solent, in a top class RIB. This can either be a taster of what you could be experiencing, or just the best birthday present for the man in your life. www.ukpowerboatcharter.com. Or try www.boatability.co.uk.

Shared Ownership

Half way between chartering for the day, and outright ownership is shared ownership. Here the ownership of the boat is split into shares, typically between four and twelve, which give you between one month and three months of usage every year. The main advantage is reduced first cost, followed closely by reduced annual costs, with the moorings, maintenance and insurance split between the owners. Usually the company arranging the deal also takes care of the management of the boat, for a fixed fee, removing this headache. Other similar schemes offer you annual weeks in a variety of different boats, power and sail.

Chapter 2:
Buying your boat

**New or secondhand? Boat show, magazine or on online?
We look at how and where you buy your first boat**

So now you have a reasonable idea of the size and type of boat you are thinking about, it is time to start looking.

The first decision you need to make is do you want a new boat or secondhand?

Buying new

A new boat gives you the obvious benefit of reliability, with a warranty back-up if there are any breakdowns. You will be able to choose the specification of your boat, plus details such as colour and trim. Most new craft come with a long list of options, and you need to be aware of these, especially when you are comparing prices.

Firstly and most importantly you will need to decide on the engine size and type. Most new boats will have more than one power option, plus

possibly the choice of outboard or inboard, petrol or diesel. A more powerful engine will give you a higher top speed. It will also allow you to carry a greater load comfortably. This will depend on the number of passengers you are regularly going to have on board, and the amount of gear, but more importantly the amount of fuel. If you are regularly going to be traveling long distances, with full fuel and equipment, you will need more power, to get the boat on the plane, and keep it running comfortably. Equally, if the kids are wanting to wakeboard you will need a bigger engine. But if you are normally only going to be travelling with two of you, you will need less power than if your party is six large adults.

Petrol versus diesel used to be easy. Petrol engines were cheaper to buy, lighter, gave you more speed, but cost

significantly more to run. This is partly because diesels are 10-20% more efficient, but more importantly because marine diesel used to be tax free, costing less than half the price of petrol. Therefore the more miles you were likely to cover in a year, the better option a diesel became. Since 2009 however pump prices are almost identical, so the decision is harder. Up to 20-23ft, petrols still probably score on performance and first cost, whereas above 27ft diesels rule. In between will depend on how much you are going to use your boat, and how far you will travel each year.

Some outboard-powered boats will be available without an engine, allowing you to fit your own if you have already got one, or buy one from an engine distributor. However before going down this route be quite clear of

Below: Boat Shows allow you to see the largest number of new boats in a day. On-water shows like The Southampton Boat Show allow you to test-drive many of the craft

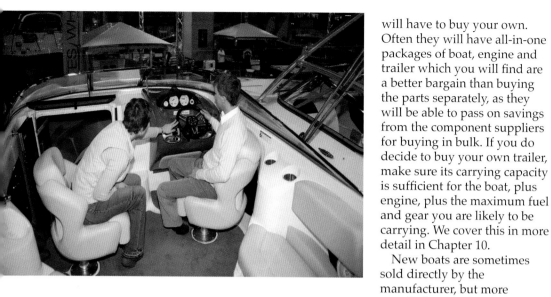

will have to buy your own. Often they will have all-in-one packages of boat, engine and trailer which you will find are a better bargain than buying the parts separately, as they will be able to pass on savings from the component suppliers for buying in bulk. If you do decide to buy your own trailer, make sure its carrying capacity is sufficient for the boat, plus engine, plus the maximum fuel and gear you are likely to be carrying. We cover this in more detail in Chapter 10.

New boats are sometimes sold directly by the manufacturer, but more usually by a dealer. He will buy products from the manufacturer, show them at boat shows, advertise them in magazines, and demonstrate them. The better ones will also be able to offer you finance packages, training, and servicing of the boat through its life. He will handle warranty claims, though ultimately these will be covered by the maker.

Some makes will have just one dealer per country, some will have multiple dealerships, in different areas. Some will have agreements whereby individual dealers will just handle enquiries from their area, though even so you are free to go to whichever one you wish. You don't even have to go to the dealer in your country, or the country you will be boating in. Many British people who keep their boats in the Mediterranean for instance will buy them in the UK. However in general you should

our capabilities of fitting an engine. Anything over 10hp requires specialist knowledge and equipment, and can be potentially dangerous if you get it wrong. Also remember that the dealer will often be able to offer you a package price that is as good as you will get from buying the two separately.

After the engine you will be offered a whole host of options, depending on the size of the boat. With small craft it will possibly be just a question of do you want a cover, or cushions for the seats. Larger cruisers will include options in the galley - cooker, fridge, hot and cold water, and in the cabin - stereo, tables, curtains, holding tanks for the toilet. Externally you can have different gelcoat colours, adjustable seats and steering wheel, bathing platform, ski-pole, tonneau cover or camper canvas and so on. More extended cruising in

the biggest boats may also need an anchor windlass to help you pull up the ground tackle. This can be either manual or electric.

You will also be needing a trailer if you are going to be towing your boat. Sometimes the dealer may be able to supply this, otherwise you

Right: This sportscruiser has a large cockpit, and accommodation under the fore-deck

be careful about bringing in boats from abroad, as you may find the local If there are no shows coming up, dealer less willing to look after it should it go wrong. There may also be warranty implications.

If there is more than one dealer, you may find it worthwhile shopping around, as they may have some better offers on individual boats they have in stock, but this may not always prove a good move in the long run as we will discuss next.

Discounts can be a problem area in the boating business. To put them in context, most makers will set a List Price, or Recommended Retail Price for each model. The dealer will buy boats at a trade discount from this price. He will then sell them for somewhere between the two. The difference between his buying and selling price covers his overheads - staff costs, premises, boat shows and advertising. In theory most manufacturers suggest their dealers stick to the list prices, but in practice, and by law, there is nothing compelling them to do this.

However, looking for the best discount is not always a good idea. A boat is not like a washing machine, that you buy, put in the kitchen and then don't look at till it stops working ten years later, at which point you buy a new one. Boats are complicated, need careful maintenance and looking after, and as you use

Above and Right: Secondhand boats make a good buy, if they have been well looked after. This is the author's 4m Avon Searider, 25 years old when it was bought, and a bargain at £2500 including engine and trailer, but you need to know what you are looking for on a boat of this age, and should go for newer boats (right) if you are not an expert

them over the years, you often need back-up and help from the dealer. How much he is prepared and able to do this will depend on how much profit he made from the sale. A low price, low overhead dealer may not have the staff and facilities to deal your questions and problems.

At the same time, he may be offering an extra discount on a model simply because it is one that he has in stock, or that he is having difficulty selling. Because of this it may not be the right boat for you. A RIB with the smallest option engine on it may be being offered at a good discount, but if you are going to have four adults regularly with you, or kids who want to waterski, it will prove to be a poor bargain. And when you come to sell it, you will find no-one else wants it.

And of course you have to remember that if every customer is being offered the same high discounts, the re-sale values of all that range of boats will be correspondingly lowered.

This brings us to the downside of buying new, depreciation. All boats will lose value as soon as they are sold. This depreciation is not so severe as with cars, but you can still expect to lose 10-20% in the first one to two years. After that the rate of fall slows, but still continues, until gradually, after ten years or so it reaches a plateau. Re-sale values are

also affected by the make and model, with popular boats and models holding their values better, and the engines, with diesels commanding better long-term prices, though at the expense of higher first costs.

To find your new boat, the best starting point is a boat show. This will allow you to walk around all the makes and types, and get a feel of what you are looking for. The two largest shows are London in January, and Southampton in September. In between is the new Powerboat & RIB Show at Portsmouth in May, and the Beale Park Boat Show in June.

A show will allow you to compare boats, talk to the dealers, and get aboard them, sometimes on test runs. Nothing equals actually stepping aboard to get a feel for what you want. You may also pick up show bargains, but don't rush into these, unless you have done your research already, and know what you want. If you talk to the dealer, and sound like a good customer, they will probably hold the price for a month or so after.

Shows also give you an idea of the operation the dealer runs. Look for professionalism, sales staff who are helpful and interested, but not pushy, and who are prepared to listen to what you want. Tell them how much you want to spend, where you are going to be boating, and how much

experience you have. Beware being offered cut-price bargains before they even know what will be best for you. Many dealers will then run open days shortly after the show, which will give you the opportunity to actually try out the boats.

If there are no shows coming up, then the next source of company information is in magazines. Titles like Powerboat & RIB Magazine, Motorboats Monthly, and Motorboat & Yachting run regular reviews.

Once you have found the companies that appear to be offering what you want, get their brochures go along to their premises and see the boats and when you are getting close to making your decision, ask them for a test drive, on the boat you want, or one similar. Don't expect them to launch every new boat from their showroom, but they should have a representative model available for you to drive.

Once you have made your decision, you will be asked for deposit, usually between 10-20%, with the balance being paid on handover of the vessel. It is a good idea to ask the company where they bank this money, as it will be at risk if they go out of business between taking it and supplying you with your boat. For large purchases you will have more security if it is placed in a client account.

Right: This cuddy-
fishing boat also
makes a good
general-purpose
family day-boat

Below: On-water
shows allow you to go
out on potential boats
for short sea-trials

Surveys

If you are buying
a secondhand boat
we would strongly
recommend you
consider having it
surveyed before
you purchase.
On a boat over
£10,000 bought
from a broker
or privately this
is a must. Over
£5,000 it is
advisable if you
are not sure about
your expertise in
spotting faults.

Most UK
surveyors
belong to the
Yacht Designers
and Surveyors
Association, www.
ydsa.co.uk, who
will give you a list
of their members
local to you or
where the boat is.

Buying secondhand

If your budget can't run
to a new boat, then don't
despair, because the majority
of people actually get afloat
in secondhand craft. Unlike
cars, boats do not wear out
significantly with age, and
secondhand does not have the
same connotation. Good used
boats are available at all prices,
but expect to pay around 50% of
the value of an equivalent new
craft and upwards, for a reliable
good condition example.

Used boats can be found
through a variety of outlets.
Firstly try the dealers
themselves, as they will often
have trade-in models for sale,
and are likely to give you a
limited warranty with these.
The next route is a broker.
These will have lists of boats
for sale, usually belonging to
existing owners, in the same
way as an estate agent sells
houses. As with a house,
you are actually buying the
boat from the owner, and the

broker merely acts as an agent,
taking no responsibility for the
condition of the craft, or the
accuracy of any statement that
the owner may make about it,
though the better companies
will still take an interest in wha
is said, and try to prevent any
obvious misrepresentations.

Brokers advertise in
magazines. They can also be
found on the internet. Some
boats may appear on the books
of more than one broker, again
in the same way as a house. Th
broker will arrange for you to
see over the boat, which may
be at their premises or marina,
or elsewhere, and will set up
a test drive. They will take
any offer you may make, and
pass it on to the owner. If you
agree a price, they will take a
deposit, usually 10%, though
again you should ask where
this is banked. The broker also
takes the final payment, then
deducts a commission, usually
somewhere between 8-10%,
before passing the balance on
to the owner. The of using a
broker is that they can arrange
inspections at any time, withou
the owner having to be there.
They will also often have more
than one similar boat on their
books.

The next option is to buy
privately, dealing directly with
the owner. Private sales, can be
found in the classified pages o
magazines, on the internet on
specialist websites, and in you

about your qualifications, you should get a survey carried out professionally. For boats under £5,000 this may be disproportionately expensive, but over this price it is worth considering, and over £10,000 a definite. The survey will usually pick up enough points for you to haggle with the seller and recoup the cost. Having said that, any secondhand boat will show signs of wear, and be in need of some work doing on it, so you can't claim for everything. And again, if the seller says he can't wait for you to get a survey, then walk away, because there is probably a problem he is wanting to hide.

When looking at the boat, ask for any proof of work that has been done. If the engine has been serviced recently, as

ocal newspaper. You may also ind private boats on marina noticeboards, and of course here is the ubiquitous eBay, with growing numbers of boats or sale here of all types.

When buying privately, you will have to arrange to inspect it at a time convenient to yourself and the owner. Again if you agree a price, but can't take the boat away at the time, or want to arrange a survey, then you can leave a deposit, but you must make it quite clear, in writing, the basis on which you are doing this. Simply changing your mind later will not entitle you to your money ack. Normally it is stated as being subject to a satisfactory urvey, or confirmation of ome of the details. At the same ime you need to be quite clear xactly what you are buying. Does it include the trailer, loose quipment on the boat, such as opes, fenders, lifejackets? Write own a list, and better still, ake a couple of photographs. f the seller starts to query this, nen walk away from the deal. Remember, you don't have to uy it.

Surveys

When looking at any boat, it is ital that you get a good idea f its condition, and that of ne engine and equipment. If ou are not an expert yourself, ake along a friend who nows about boats. If in doubt

Above: Brokers will have more than one boat available for you to look at

Right: package deals of boat, engine and possibly trailer will save you money

it should, there should be an invoice. A good owner will have kept all the bills over the years.

Proof of ownership

One of the most difficult questions with any used boat is proving the seller is its real owner, and more importantly that there are no outstanding debts or loans on it. Unlike a car, a boat does not have a registration document, and there is no central agency such as the DVLA with records of all craft. It is therefore down to you to assure yourself that the seller is bona fide, and the boat has not been stolen. Simple checks include asking for the invoice from the previous sale to that person, or the name and address of the previous owner. Ask for confirmation of insurance for the past and previous years. Ask for receipts for any work that has been done, or items that have been bought. Ask for receipts for mooring or launching. Obviously you have to drop this carefully into the conversation, as you don't wish to spoil the relationship with the seller, but a bona fide owner will have all this information to hand, and should in fact be offering it to you. Again if none of this is available, or he says he is selling it for friend, start feeling suspicious. If you buy a stolen boat, and the real owner tracks it down, you lose

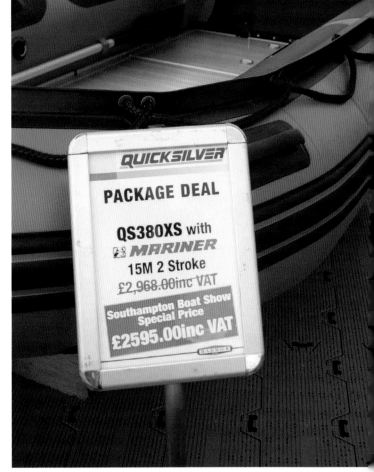

everything.

Loans or debts on the boat are much harder to pin down, but if it is being held as security for a loan or marine mortgage, and you buy it, the creditor will have first claim over the boat to recover the debt owing. About all you can do is get the seller to state on the receipt or sale document that to his

knowledge there is no debt outstanding on the boat. At least this gives you some basis on which to, pursue him if it later transpires to be untrue.

And if all this sounds very off-putting, you should remember that cases of fraudulent boat sales are comparatively rare. Just make sure you aren't one of them.

Buying Tips

irst and foremost you are looking for a boat that has been looked after. Neglect and ack of maintenance are more damaging to a boat than careful use. But this is as much ntuition as detail inspection. Is it clean. Are the mooring ropes in good condition, or rayed and dirty. Is the canopy clean, or is it green, frayed and with broken fasteners. When you open the cabin door, do you get a clean fresh smell, or a musty odour. Are the arpets clean. Is the joinery shining and polished, or dark and scratched. Look for stains nder the windows and portlights – a sure sign of leaks, or in the overhead lining.

RIBs RIB tubes are attacked from above nd below. From above the invisible enemy UV radiation. This will gradually degrade he material, attacking some more than thers. Hypalon tubes will last longer han PVC and are a definite buying plus. n overall cover not only keeps the boat lean and dry, it will stop the harmful rays. nderneath, check the tube-to-hull join, specially from midships forward, where ounding from head seas can tear it free. Seats, consoles and grabrails take a ammering from the weight of people anging onto them as the boat hits the aves. Check fastenings, and the GRP hrough which they are secured.

Engine The engine and its fixings take a ounding as the boat jumps from the waves. heck the transom bracket for cracks or orrosion. Check the through-bolts are ecure. Check the transom in way of the olts for stress-cracks, and where it joins he hull bottom and sides. Run the engine, heck for smooth tick-over, and good flow

of cooling water from the tell-tale. Check the power trim operates all the way up. Check the steering is smooth and free, with no backlash. Check fuel lines, filter and tank for leaks or corrosion. You should ask to hear the engine running if the boat is ashore, but before you buy it is essential to go for a full-throttle run.

Check that the engines and stern-drives have been regularly and recently serviced, with new anodes fitted, and don't be afraid to ask to see invoices to prove this. A cared-for boat will have all these documents, and the broker or owner should have them to show you. Check the aluminium casing is not corroded. The power trim rams should be shiny and clean. Lift the leg to check for wear in the joints. Check the bellows are still flexible and not cracked. Once they crack, water gets into the drive-train, with disastrous results.

Trailer The main areas to look at are the bearings and brakes. These suffer from salt-water corrosion if they have not been

flushed out after launching. As a minimum, jack up one side and spin the wheel(s). If they sound noisy, the bearings need replacing. Check the winch is working correctly. Pull the strap out to its full extent to look for chafing. Check the tyres are not perished or damaged. Check the load capacity on the maker's plate is equal or greater than the all-up weight of the boat, fuel and gear.

Hull The hull can suffer from damage when driving into waves, or grounding on beaches or slipways. Check the spray rails for stress cracking, and the underside of the keel. Beware a boat that has been recently anti-fouled - this may hide cracks.

Electrics and instruments

Instruments and electronics will be exposed to spray and rain, and subsequent corrosion. Check they all work. A console cover will give protection.

It is not that any of these faults cannot be put right, and just one or two should not put you off buying a boat, but they do give a good general indication of whether it has been looked after, how much the owner has cared for it, and how much work you are going to have to do after you buy it. If you are in any doubt, get a survey, or walk away from the deal – there are plenty of other boats out there.

RIBEX the Rib Show at Cowes is now moving to Gunwharf Quays Portsmouth in May 2012, and will be called The Powerboat & RIB Show, with many more boats than RIBs there

"If you were considering spending £20k + on a new boat - wouldn't you want some input into the design?"

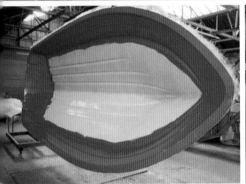

The Fletcher Difference

You can find your choices compromised when dealing with a number of resellers.

It can be a case of *"Any colour you like – provided it's the one we have in stock!"*

Considering the investment required for new boats we think you should be able to have a significant input into the end product.

As a manufacturer, not only do we offer an extensive choice of in-gel colour options but you are also free to mix and match. Choose your own hull, topsides and deck combination.

Match this to a choice of literally 100's of upholstery colours, textures and patterns to create a boat that is truly unique.

You even have the option to sit down with our in-house team and create your own custom interior and pick from an extensive range of components and fittings to complete the package to your own exacting standards.

We will always be on hand to help and advise.

Once you have decided on your perfect boat we can supply you with regular pictures as she goes through the build process – you can even come to the factory yourself to see how she is put together.

Every boat is water tested to ensure engines and systems are working 100%. Those new to boating can benefit from an on-the-water handover than includes basic boat handling and launch/recovery skills.

To experience the Fletcher Difference please contact one of our team members who would be happy to help.

Boat Packages from: £12,890.00 to £32,190.00

For more information on the range and history of our boats check out:
www.fletcher-boats.co.uk

fletcher

wolverhampton, west midlands, WV6 9H
0845 230 56

Left: The modern four-stroke outboard is an extremely sophisticated piece of engineering. This 5.3-litre 350hp V8 has twin overhead camshafts per bank, operating four-valves per cylinder

CHAPTER 3:
Engines

**Which size and type of engine is the best for your boat?
Tony Jones guides you through the different options,
and explains the mysteries that lie under the hood**

As with a new car, you will be faced with several engine options with your new boat, and it is important that you choose the right one for how you intend to use it, but just as important is to choose the engine that other people will want, so you don't have problems when you come to sell it.

You may be offered a choice of petrol or diesel, and perhaps two or three different horsepowers. Some boats may even offer you outboard or stern-drive power. In this chapter we will guide you through the different options, to enable you to make the right choice.

When buying secondhand you will have to take the engine that comes with the boat, of course. But an understanding of the various types of engine available is important to make sure you get the package that best suits your needs.

Engine types

The different types of engines and transmissions used by sportsboats and small cruisers can appear confusing, but most of them have a lot in common.

Firstly we should be clear that by engine we mean the block that produces the power, just as in your car, and by transmission we mean the

The carburettor two-stroke cycle

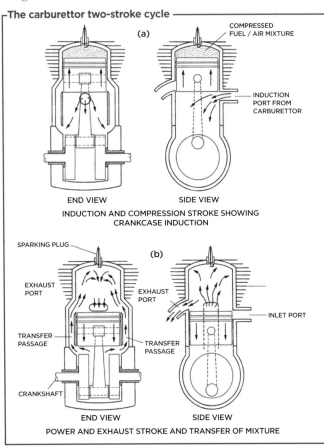

(a)

COMPRESSED FUEL / AIR MIXTURE

INDUCTION PORT FROM CARBURETTOR

END VIEW · SIDE VIEW

INDUCTION AND COMPRESSION STROKE SHOWING CRANKCASE INDUCTION

SPARKING PLUG

(b)

EXHAUST PORT

EXHAUST PORT

INLET PORT

TRANSFER PASSAGE

TRANSFER PASSAGE

CRANKSHAFT

END VIEW · SIDE VIEW

POWER AND EXHAUST STROKE AND TRANSFER OF MIXTURE

Above: The carburetor two-stroke cycle

Opposite page: Cutaway drawing of a two-cylinder four-stroke outboard

gears and shafts that connect the engine to the propeller and allows that power to be converted into thrust.

The basic principles of boat engines - four-stroke, two-stroke, petrol and diesel are the same as in your car or motorbike, and indeed, many are adaptations (marinised versions, as they're known) of existing engines used in cars and other road vehicles. But there's a much wider variation in the way they are installed. Let's look at the basic categories: inboard, outboard, sterndrive (also known as outdrive), surface-drive, and waterjet.

Inboard

The inboard arrangement usually puts the engine roughly in the middle of the boat with a very simple forward and reverse gearbox directly attached to the rear end of the crankshaft. The

drive to the propeller consists of a shaft that goes out through the bottom of the boat at a shallow angle, with the propeller itself directly bolted on the end. The rudder, which steers the boat, is separate and works by deflecting the thrust from the prop to one side or the other.

A bracket supports the shaft immediately in front of the prop. This is layout is referred to as conventional inboard or shaft drive. In a few cases the engine is reversed, with a vee-drive gearbox attached to its forward end. This is more expensive, but compact.

The propeller shaft, its support bracket, and the rudder create a considerable amount of drag. Also the thrust is at an angle from the horizontal. This gives a lower propulsive efficiency than a sterndrive or outboard, the other popular alternatives, so will always be a bit slower for

Two-Strokes and Four-Strokes

Until very recently, the internal combustion engine came in two basic formats - two-stroke and four-stroke. These days there are three as Direct Injection, or DI two-strokes differ so widely from the original type to justify having a class of their own. With boats, two-stroke technology is found only in outboard motors; there are no inboard or sterndrive two-strokes. But this technology has long been used in many other non-marine applications, the most common being for those little mopeds, scooters and chainsaws - the sort with an exhaust note like an angry wasp.

So let's look at the pros and cons of the two types of two-stroke and the entirely different four-stroke.

In the two-stroke the engine fires once every revolution. During this time the piston has gone down once and up once, ie two strokes. In the four-stroke the engine fires once every two revolutions. During this time the piston has therefore gone down twice and up twice, ie four-strokes.

Thus the two-stroke can in theory deliver twice the power for an equivalent engine capacity and rpm. However, the limitations caused by the power stroke being combined with the

exhaust and inlet mean that some of the available power is lost, as is some of the fuel, which escapes unburnt. For this reason the two-stroke is not exactly twice as powerful as the four-stroke, but more importantly it is much less efficient, with a fuel consumption nearly twice as high.

For many years the relative inefficiency of the conventional two-stroke was offset by its high power-to-weight ratio, important when the engine is being hung on the transom, and the inherent simplicity of its design. In fact its only moving parts are the piston and crankshaft, with the inlet and exhaust ports being set in the side of the

cylinder wall, opened and closed by the piston passing up and down. The four-stroke on the other hand needs valves in the cylinder head, and associated camshafts,

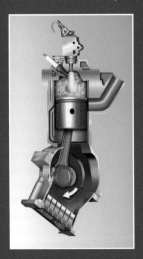

chains and rockers to open them.

This made the four-stroke heavier, and more expensive to build, and require much more extensive servicing and maintenance.

Conventional two-strokes also had to have their lubricating oil mixed with the fuel, as they had no sump as such, which further contributed to emissions they made, with the result that in 2007 the European Commission banned their use for leisure purposes. This forced most of the major manufacturers to design and build a whole new range of four-stroke engines to meet the legislation.

An alternative route

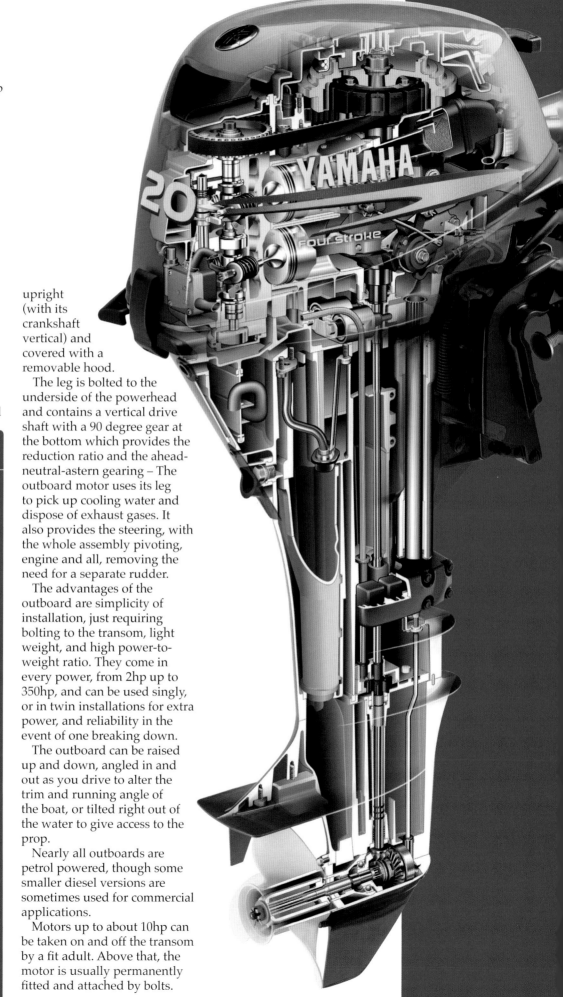

the same power.

Inboards are equally divided between petrol, and diesel, with some even being converted to run on LPG (liquid petroleum gas) for economy. Powers go from 20hp up to 500hp.

Note: Marine engine gearboxes don't have multiple gears – just forward, neutral, and reverse. However, both ahead and astern have some reduction gearing meaning that the speed of the output shaft is less than the engine speed. This is necessary because engines need to turn fast to produce power, but propellers work better when turning slower. Reduction ratios are commonly between 1.5:1 to 3:1.

Outboard Motors

Most of us understand what an outboard motor looks like. The general principle is that the engine –known in this case as the powerhead – is mounted

adopted by some makers was the direct-injection two-stroke, in which the fuel is injected into the cylinder when the piston is near the top of its stroke. This reduced the fuel wastage, to such an extent that these engines are now also allowed to be sold in Europe.

It has to be said though that much of America, and most of the rest of the world still allows sales of conventional two-strokes, reasoning possibly that the net emission contribution of a comparatively small number of outboards, used for occasional leisure trips is minute compared to the millions of mopeds used round the world every day.

However, be that as it may, today on a new boat you will be offered either a four-stroke outboard, or direct injection two-stroke. However secondhand boats with conventional two-strokes can still be bought sold, and used, and are likely to be so into the future.

upright (with its crankshaft vertical) and covered with a removable hood.

The leg is bolted to the underside of the powerhead and contains a vertical drive shaft with a 90 degree gear at the bottom which provides the reduction ratio and the ahead-neutral-astern gearing – The outboard motor uses its leg to pick up cooling water and dispose of exhaust gases. It also provides the steering, with the whole assembly pivoting, engine and all, removing the need for a separate rudder.

The advantages of the outboard are simplicity of installation, just requiring bolting to the transom, light weight, and high power-to-weight ratio. They come in every power, from 2hp up to 350hp, and can be used singly, or in twin installations for extra power, and reliability in the event of one breaking down.

The outboard can be raised up and down, angled in and out as you drive to alter the trim and running angle of the boat, or tilted right out of the water to give access to the prop.

Nearly all outboards are petrol powered, though some smaller diesel versions are sometimes used for commercial applications.

Motors up to about 10hp can be taken on and off the transom by a fit adult. Above that, the motor is usually permanently fitted and attached by bolts.

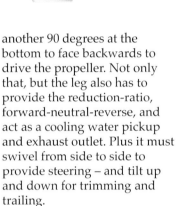

Right: The CMD Zeus is a steerable pod-drive, that takes the power from large inboard diesels out through the bottom of the boat, removing the need for prop-shaft and rudder

Below: A diesel stern-drive

Bottom: This jet-drive is excellent in shallow waters, giving a flush bottom to the boat, with no prop to get damaged, or injure swimmers

Sterndrives

The sterndrive, also know as the outdrive, was originally called the inboard / outboard because although the engine itself is in inside the hull, the transmission leg is outside and looks a bit like the vertical part of an outboard motor. This streamlined leg and absence of separate rudder gives the sterndrive a propulsive efficiency only challenged by the outboard motor, making it ideal for sportsboats so is often found on high-performance craft.

The sterndrive is the most complex of the three types as the drive from the engine has to pass through the transom, turn through 90 degrees to the vertical at the top of the leg, and then turn through another 90 degrees at the bottom to face backwards to drive the propeller. Not only that, but the leg also has to provide the reduction-ratio, forward-neutral-reverse, and act as a cooling water pickup and exhaust outlet. Plus it must swivel from side to side to provide steering – and tilt up and down for trimming and trailing.

And if all that wasn't enough, sterndrives come in two options - single-prop or twin-prop (DuoProp). You can tell the latter by its twin propellers. These rotate in opposite directions (called counter-rotating), so the lower half of the leg has the additional mechanical complication of two concentric prop shafts. Twin props are essential on bigger sterndrives, particularly diesels to get all the power and torque into the water, while keeping the overall diamtere of the props down.. They are also a favourite for single engine installations as the counter-rotating props cancel out what's known as torque steer - the tendency for a single propeller to always turn the boat in one direction even when pointing straight ahead, which has to be otherwise counteracted by slightly turning the wheel.

Because sterndrives legs are mechanically complex and often highly stressed, they do not tolerate abuse. Regular annual maintenance is essential if unreliability and expensive repairs are to be avoided – especially when coupled to a powerful diesel engine.

Pod Drive

The latest way to get your engine's power into the water is the so-called pod-drive. Like the sterndrive this uses two 90 degree gearboxes, but they emerge through the bottom of the boat not the transom. They are normally only found in diesel powers above 300hp, so you are unlikely to find them except in the larger sportscruisers. Cummins Mercruiser's Zeus, and Volvo's IPS are the two makes to look for.

Jet drive

This is the system used by all Personal Water Craft (PWCs) and Jetskis, and some smaller RIBs. Water is drawn in through an intake underneath the boat and is accelerated to high speed by an impeller running in a tubular duct before being squirted out the back. The impeller is shaft driven by an engine ahead of the duct. The outlet nozzle of the duct swivels left and right to give steering, and has a clam-shaped bucket that drops down being it to direct the water flow forward and so give reverse. The advantages of jet drives are no exposed propeller so no danger to anyone in the

Left: Twin engines give extra security for boats that are regularly going to be used offshore, or commercial craft

Below: Twin props or Duoprops give extra thrust with higher power diesel engines, and eliminate torque-steer with single petrol engines

Bottom: 9.9hp is probably the heaviest engine you can lift off a boat on your own.

vater, and a flush bottom to he boat, which means it can perate in the shallowest water. he engine is always petrol, nd can either be four-stroke r two-stroke, though with the ame restrictions on areas of se as with outboards.

A few jet drives have been tted to sportsboats, but the elative inefficiency of the drive as meant it has never caught n except in for craft in shallow vaters.

Surface drive

This is a specialised version of the inboard for very high speed applications that avoids the drag of conventional propeller shafts and brackets. It uses a drive shaft that emerges from the transom, on the waterline, with a result that the propeller is running only half immersed, giving them the name of surface propellers. The shaft has a universal joint where it passes through the transom, allowing it to swivel left and right for steering, and up and down to alter the running angle of the boat. These drives are rarely found on boats under 30ft.

Above: A 90hp four-stroke is ideal for this 18ft cuddy-cruiser

Right: This Arneson steerable surface-drive is designed for high-performance craft and racing boats

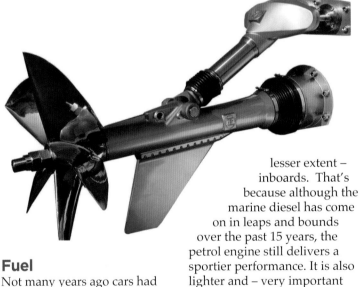

Fuel

Not many years ago cars had petrol engines and trucks had diesels. Petrol engines were smooth, clean and quiet; diesel engines rough, noisy and dirty. That's no longer true, as anyone who has driven a car with a modern diesel engine knows.

Petrol and LPG

In boats, each fuel retains its own niche to a much greater extent. For a start, all outboards run on petrol and this is the most common choice for sterndrives and – to a slightly lesser extent – inboards. That's because although the marine diesel has come on in leaps and bounds over the past 15 years, the petrol engine still delivers a sportier performance. It is also lighter and – very important for those entering the pastime – less expensive.

As with cars, marine petrol engines can be converted to run on much cheaper liquid petroleum gas (LPG) but the fuel isn't widely available in UK marinas.

Diesel

The diesel engine is still, generally speaking, heavier and bigger than a petrol engine of the same power. This makes them more expensive to buy.

Diesels are more often found in sports cruisers with at least overnight accommodation, as for this type of boat ultimate performance is less important. It is particularly popular for those that remain in the water all through the season as waterside diesel is far more widely available than petrol. In the UK, the greatly reduced flammability of diesel fuel has always been a big factor in its favour for family boating. But one of the diesel engine's most valuable characteristics, its longevity, is wasted in pleasure boats. Most diesel engines rust away long before they ever wear out.

Diesel also provides more mpg and also, in the UK, has until recently been about a third of the price of petrol as recreational boaters have been able to use lightly-taxed commercial diesel. In 2007 however, the European Union removed this concession, and from 2009 the tax on both fuels has been the same as on road forecourts . This could lead to a revival of the petrol engine for some types of boat.

Which?
one is for you

for trailing and beaching, and trimmed to improve the running angle of the boat. Frees up valuable space in the middle of the boat. Twin prop versions remove torque-steer tendencies in single engine installations.

Against: High power versions are highly stressed. Adherence to maintenance schedule absolutely essential and best done professionally every year, which can be expensive. Paint chips must be attended to and anodes replaced regularly to avoid corrosion in salt water. Replacement of twin-props expensive. Used for sportsboats, sportscruisers, and larger RIBs. Petrol versions lighter, so easier to tow, and much cheaper to buy than diesel, but use 10-15% more fuel. Petrol installations used to have a lower resale price, but the gap is now closing.

Outboard Motors

For: Enormous choice of manufacturers and power outputs from 2hp to 350hp. The only sort of engine which can be removed or changed for another without too much trouble. Portable up to about 10hp. Readily available on the secondhand market. The latest generation of high-power motors are among the most advanced and efficient internal combustion engines in the world. New four-strokes and direct-injection two-

strokes are clean, quiet and environmentally friendly. Any outboard is much lighter than the equivalent power inboard or sterndrive. It also has lower maintenance costs.

Against: Older, conventional two-strokes are powerful but less efficient, with poor fuel consumption, but cheaper to maintain. Modern four-strokes require comparatively expensive annual maintenance, but the direct-injection engines have very low maintenance costs. The ease of removal of outboards can make them targets for thieves.

nboard

For: Simplicity, robustness and ow maintenance. Prop shaft nd rudder grip the water very vell and aid manoeuvring in he marina in twin installations.

Against: Takes up room in he middle of the boat. Can e awkward to service if pace is tight. Relatively poor propulsive efficiency. Single nstallations tricky to handle vhen mooring. Propeller nd rudder vulnerable to grounding. Not very suitable or trailing. Used mainly for ski-tow boats, either petrol or LPG powered, nd some larger sportscruisers, round 30ft and upwards.

Sterndrives

For: Excellent propulsive efficiency. Can be tilted up

Below: Direct-injection two-strokes are the latest technology, giving light weight, and reduced maintenance compared to a four-stroke

Right: Chandleries are the shops where you buy your boating gear. You can also buy online, but nothing beats actually seeing what you are getting, trying it out before you buy, and asking advice from the staff

Chapter 4:
Equipping your boat

Below: The choice of ropes is often bewildering, but most of these are used by our sailing brothers, and the requirements of a motorboat are much simpler. But it still pays to take the advice of the chandler

Now you have bought your boat you need to kit it out. We describe the extra equipment you are likely to need for safety and comfort

Before you set off on your first trip, there are certain essential items of equipment you will need for safe boating, and a lot of other gear you can buy to make life easier and more comfortable afloat. A new boat may come with a basic starter package of equipment already supplied, but will still need more gear, while a secondhand craft may have a ragbag of bits, whose condition is questionable. You should always check these carefully, and if in doubt replace them with new, as failures may be at best inconvenient, at worst dangerous.

Boating gear is usually bought from chandleries, either shops by the waterside, or online, while boat shows provide another source of supply, often at special prices. You can also find equipment at boat jumbles, but beware, as its condition is often unknown, as is its provenance - these are often where stolen goods turn up. Always ask to see a receipt, or some proof as to where the seller acquired the item.

Ropes

Every boat should have at least two mooring lines. Typically these should be at least 22-25ft long (7-8m), or 1.5 times the length of the boat, and at least 12mm diameter, except for the smallest inflatable. In addition, on boats over 20ft, if you are traveling farther afield, a 10m line is useful as a spring or a long mooring line against high harbour walls.

Rope comes in many

different styles, colours and materials. It can be plaited or three-strand, and made from nylon, polyester or polyproplene. Nylon has slightly more stretch in it, so is more shock-absorbing for a mooring line for a larger boat. But polyester does not harden so much with exposure to the sun, making it easier to handle. Polypropylene floats, making it ideal for ski-lines, but is less strong, and harder on your hands. Plaited ropes are easier to grip, and often more colourful.

Often the choice is down to what you feel most comfortable handling, or even what matches the colour scheme of your boat providing it is the right type! Don't bother with Kevlar or pre-stretched polyester, as these are strictly for the yachties.

Anchor

You may not have been thinking about anchoring in your sportsboat, but you should always carry one nonetheless, plus an appropriate length of rope and chain. In an emergency, if your engine breaks down, an anchor will prevent you from drifting onto a rocky shore, or away from safety, or into a busy shipping lane. It will also allow you to stop off the beach if you have arrived back at the slipway at too low a state of the tide. But more pleasurably, it will allow you to stop in a sheltered bay or cove for the afternoon, without drifting into the beach, or getting stranded if the tide goes down.

Anchors come in a multitude of types, all making great claims about their holding capacity. The triangular spade or Danforth type is probably the best allrounder, with the plough type, and Bruce type giving a similar performance, but less easy to stow. They are measured by their weight, with the heavier the anchor, the bigger and heavier boat it will hold safely in place without dragging.

Again your chandler will advise on the best size for your particular boat, but as an approximate guide, for a sportsboat up to 18ft (5.5m) 5kg

will suffice. Up to 21ft (6.5m) 7kg, and 25ft (7.5m), 9kg.

You then need sufficient line, plus a length of chain between it and the anchor to give extra weight, and keep the pull horizontal. 2m of chain, plus 20m of nylon line, either 10mm or 12mm will normally be sufficient for inshore cruising. Bigger boats going further offshore will need a heavier anchor, and more line.

The neatest packages comprise an anchor, chain and line, all in a strong bag, keeping them tidy and ready for use.

Always make sure the end of the line is permanently secured to a strong point at the bow of the boat - there is nothing more stupid than throwing the anchor overboard, then watching the line disappear.

Lifejackets

A lifejacket for everyone who may be aboard at any time is an absolute must. When you wear them is ultimately the decision of the skipper, but our advice is always wear them at all times.

Lifejackets in fact come in two forms, lifejackets and buoyancy aids, both of which are covered by European legislation. This requires testing to approved standards, and the weight of person they are suitable for, plus the CE mark shown on them. A lifejacket is designed to keep you afloat with your head above the water, and to turn you over on your back should you fall in unconscious. It will have crutch straps to prevent it riding up. A buoyancy aid is designed to a lower specification, and will help keep you afloat, but not turn you over. However because it is less bulky, it is sometimes worn by waterskiers, or any situation where a rescue boat is close at hand.

Our advice is always buy full lifejackets. These can come in two forms - either with permanent foam buoyancy in place, or inflatable versions. The inflatable lifejackets are less bulky, less obtrusive, and can be comfortably worn at all times. They look like a large pair of braces when deflated. Manual inflatable models have

to be blown up by mouth, but we would always recommend you buy the automatic inflating variety. These have a small CO2 gas cylinder, which activates immediately on contact with water. Thus you will be turned over, and held afloat, even if you should bang your head when falling overboard.

Make sure everyone knows how to put their lifejacket on, and it is properly adjusted. Keep them safe and dry, and check them every year for tears or damage, and replace the gas cylinder at the manufacturer's recommended intervals.

Paddle

A paddle, or better still two is a good idea on small to mid-size boats, should your engine fail. You won't make much progress, but it may make the difference between floating into danger. Telescopic versions take up least room.

Fenders

These are inflated plastic balls used to protect your boat from damage when tied up to a pontoon or wall, or to prevent damaging another boat if you come alongside. Even RIBs, with their rubber tubes need to carry some to prevent chafing or punctures. You should have at least three, preferably four, and they can be either round or sausage shape.

The size will depend on the length of your boat - choose what looks appropriate, or check what similar craft in the marina are using.

Boathook

Handy for picking up a mooring buoy, or anything that has dropped overboard, and for pulling yourself into the pontoon if you have not quite got your approach right. Again the telescopic aluminium variety takes up least room.

Far Right: Flares
are used to attract
attention in an
emergency

Bailer and bucket

You are always going to get
water onboard, especially in
a RIB. Even if it has a bilge-
pump, the last inch or so will
slosh around your feet. A
dinghy bailer and sponge will
get rid of this, while a bucket
always comes in handy for
cleaning.

Fire extinguishers

All new boats should come
with the appropriate fire
extinguishers, but if not
you should fit at least one,
preferably two, depending on
the size of the craft. Boats with
enclosed engine compartments
should have one mounted in
here, operated automatically
in case of fire, and one manual
one easily reached from the
helm. Fit it next to the door of
a cabin, not at the far end.

First Aid Kit

Always carry an appropriate
size first aid box on board, kept
in a dry locker.

Tool Kit

Make yourself up a kit of basic
tools that you might need to
enable you to carry out simple
repairs, carried in a plastic box.
As a minimum include pliers,
screw-drivers, mole-grips,
spanners, large adjustable
spanner, sharp knife, plus spare
bulbs for the nav lights. Add to
this some electrical connectors
and rolls of tape. These should
include duck tape - and always
buy the genuine variety, not
cheap car boot offerings,
as they are not so strong or
waterproof, insulating tape,
and self-amalgamating tape,
or rescue tape. This latter can
be used to mend leaking hoses,
or make waterproof electrical
joints. As an extra include a
small socket set.

Torches

Carry at least two waterproof
torches on board. One small
one for working on board,
and a large one for spotting at
night, or attracting attention.
Rechargeable torches are
becoming popular, but their
batteries will gradually
discharge, rendering them
useless when you need them,
unless you can recharge them
from a socket onboard. At least

one torch should have non-
rechargeable, alkali batteries,
for the longest shelf life, plus a
set of spare batteries.

Flares

A set of flares is a must for
any boat that goes to sea. They
are used to attract attention
should you get into difficulties,
and to guide rescue services
to yourself. They are usually

Right: The kill-cord
cuts the engine
ignition should the
helmsman be thrown
across the boat, or
out of it. Always carry
a spare on board,
and show passengers
where it is kept, so
they can re-start the
engine and come and
pick you up!

Spare kill-cord

The kill-cord is the device
that shuts down the engine
if the driver falls overboard,
by breaking the ignition
circuit. It is a vital piece
of safety equipment, but
how many people carry
a spare. Without it you
cannot start the engine. If
you get down to the boat
and find you have left it in
the pocket of your other
jacket, hanging up at home,
you are stranded. Or more
importantly, if the helmsman
has gone overboard, with
the cord still attached to him,
how does anyone else on
board restart the engine to
go and pick him up? Always
carry a spare, but keep it out
of sight, so the casual thief
cannot use it to take the boat.

sold in watertight packs, with
the contents appropriate to
the distance you are away
from land. The Inshore Pack
is suitable if you are travelling
up to 3 miles from land. It
comprises two orange smoke
flares, for daylight use, and two
red flares for use at night. The
Coastal pack is suitable up to 7
miles from land, and comprises
two smoke, two red, and two
parachute flares. The Offshore
pack has two smoke, four red,
and four parachute flares.

Additionally for the smallest
RIB, or personal watercraft you

Sea Start

This is a breakdown service that will come out and restart your engine if it should stop. It is a privately operated service, that you pay an annual subscription for, and noting to do with the RNLI or national rescue services. The principal area of coverage is the UK South Coast, from Chichester to Falmouth, plus shoreside services in the Channel Islands and north of France. Costs start from £140.
www.seastart.co.uk

an buy min-flare kits, which re up to nine red flares, and an be carried in your jacket.

In all cases, you should amiliarise yourself and your rew with the operation of he flares, and when you hould use them. Under no ircumstances should you set ne off, except in an emergency, nd take great care at all mes, as these are potentially angerous pyrotechnics, and ot fireworks or toys.

Keep them safe and dry, and eady to hand, not buried in a ocker. Check the expiry date, nd when they are out of date, ontact your nearest oastguard Office r information on isposal.

Charts

Paper charts of the area you are going to be boating in are a must. They allow you to plan your trip at home, and keep track of where you are afloat. They show safe channels, depths of water, and dangers. The waterproof type are the best for an open boat, with the Admiralty Leisure Tough Charts covering most of the popular cruising areas.

Electronic chart-plotters we cover in Chapter 6

Books and Guides

There are a whole range of books covering every aspect of boating, plus guides to various regions, with details of harbours and anchorages. Publishers of these include Adlard Coles, Imray, Fernhurst, and the RYA.

Spare Fuel

No matter how good you think your fuel gauge is, they are not 100% reliable or accurate, and running out is the commonest call-out for the emergency services. Carry at least two spare gallons on a small boat, five on a larger craft.

Clothing

Wearing the right clothing is essential for safe, enjoyable boating. However warm it might seem ashore, out at sea it can quickly get cold and wet, while just travelling at 30 knots adds it own wind-chill on the hottest day, reducing the temperature by 15 degrees C. If you and your passengers are not kitted out for this, the trip will quickly become unpleasant.

A good waterproof, windproof coat is the first essential. The specialist marine clothing companies make whole ranges of these, in different styles and colours, for men, women and children, and for every type of boating. Or you can go for the better quality walking gear, but this won't necessarily offer complete protection in

GPS

GPS, or Global Positioning System, uses satellites to fix your position, as with the Satnav in your car. The simplest handheld versions are still useful to check exactly where you are, but need to be used in conjunction with a paper chart. Alternatively you can buy a chart plotter, which displays your position on a screen. We describe these in more detail in Chapter 6.

Right: You can even get an app for your iPhone with the Collision Regulations on it!

the saltwater environment. Always choose breathable materials, otherwise you will quickly get clammy with sweat underneath.

The level of protection you need will depend on the type of boating you will be doing. On a fast open RIB in exposed offshore conditions you will need more than in an enclosed sportsboat, while on a jet-ski you will need something else completely. Try the jackets on before you buy, and make sure you are wearing the clothing you will normally have on underneath.

Check the hood, and make sure you can move your head around easily with it on. Closable cuffs will stop water being driven up your arms at speed. Check the pockets are big enough, and can

either be closed, or are deep enough to prevent things falling out. Remember that you will be sitting down most of the time you will be needing protection. One or more deep inside pocket is essential for your phone or handheld VHF.

Waterproof trousers are the next requirement however most people will probably only need these   on the most

VHF Radio

We describe the purpose of a radio in detail in Chapter 6, but it is worth mentioning briefly here. This is the main means of communication used between all vessels, pleasure and commercial, and land-based stations, such as coastguards, harbour-masters, port authorities and marinas. VHF (Very High Frequency) is the transmission used, and you can either have a fixed set, or portable. A portable unit is the cheapest and simplest, costing from around £75 upwards. Go for the waterproof versions, and better still floating models, in case you drop them overboard. The Lowrance floating handheld even includes a GPS positioning system, which we describe next. However, before you use a VHF, you must pass a test and get a licence, as we describe in Chapter 6.

Waterproof cases and bags

In an open boat, everything is bound to get wet at some time. It may be spray, it may be rain, or you may just drop things getting aboard. But planning for this means packing things in waterproof bags. You can get special waterproof cases for your mobile phone, VHF radio, camera or camcorder, often allowing you to operate these through clear plastic. For larger items waterproof bags will take spare clothes, books, towels, and larger electronics such as cameras, radios, iPods and binoculars. Look around at boat shows, or go to **www. aquapac.net** Aquapac, who specialise in this equipment.

exposed trips, so they can be less sophisticated, with a cheap pair sufficing. Or the semi-waterproof walking trousers make a good compromise for keeping off occasional spray.

Correct shoes or boots are vital. Best are the specialist marine types. They give good grip on wet decks, and are usually waterproof and warm. However this quality does not come cheap, and for general wear, good quality trainers, with a good wet-grip sole will often suffice. Flip-flops and slip-ons are definitely out. Keep them for the beach, but not aboard, where you need safe, secure footing. Deck shoes will normally be enough for most boating, but in an open RIB, with water sloshing about, and the chance that you may have to jump over the side at the slipway, a pair of breathable boots will keep you warm and dry, and quickly get to feel like a second skin.

For extreme RIB boating, an all-in-one suit gives the best protection, while for serious jet-skiers, a dry suit is a must.

Don't forget the humble woolly hat. It is quick and cheap, and will keep your head warm. The booming ski market means that the thinsulate variety can be picked up these days for a few pounds, together with semi-waterproof insulated gloves. Keep a couple of pair of these in a waterproof bag in a locker for when the weather should turn cold.

A peaked cap is useful for keeping the sun out of your eyes, though it needs to be a tight fit or it will blow off. Similarly a pair of sun glasses always kept on board is important, as glare off the water can double the brightness of the sun. For hot-shot RIB runners, a pair of ski-goggles will keep the sun and wind out of your eyes at 50 knots or more, and even if you don't go this fast, they will certainly look cool in the marina, and impress your passengers.

Ensign
And finally, don't forget to fly the flag. This not only shows the country you come from, it looks just that bit more professional.

The only correct flag for most British boats is the Red Ensign, flown from the stern. Don't hoist the Union Jack please, or you will get arrested. Or the Cross of St George, or the Welsh Dragon or Scottish flag. However patriotic they may seem, the law of the sea is quite clear, and there is a potential £5,000 fine if you break the rules, quite apart from looking like you don't know what you are doing.

Make sure the staff is secure in the socket, with a self-tapping screw for good measure, as it can vibrate out at speed, and don't forget to lower the flag at dusk, or you will incur the wrath of the retired-Admiral moored next to you.

Extra Items
The following should also be added to your final checklist for longer passages:

PLB Personal Locator Beacon
Radar Reflector
Spare Glasses
Jump Starter
Flask of Coffee
Water - not Alcohol
Liferaft
Engine Spares
Emergency Nav Lights

Join the RNLI
Hopefully you will never need to be rescued, but if you do, the RNLI are there to come to your aid at all times day and night, no matter what the conditions. But this magnificent service is entirely crewed by volunteers, paid for by voluntary donations. On average lifeboats are called out over 9,000 times a year, rescuing 10,000 people, over half of whom are pleasure boat users. It costs £125m to run the organisation, so why not make your contribution by joining today. For £28 a year you get their quarterly magazine, or for £68 you get in addition their Offshore Magazine, with practical and technical information, and safety advice for all forms of boating. Even if you never use them, you are helping save the lives of someone else on the water, so sign up today. **www.rnli.org.uk**

Lifejackets
when should you wear them?

Right: Get your kids into the habit of wearing a lifejacket or buoyancy aid at all times. These budding racers would never go afloat without them.

As far as the RNLI is concerned the simple answer to this question is always. They are presently running a campaign pointing out that a lifejacket is no use unless you are wearing it, and in most circumstances they are right. As you tumble off the bow in darkness into 20ft of cold water, it is no comfort to know that there is a brand-new EC Approved lifejacket safely in the cabin locker. But there are other occasions when the skipper thinks they are not necessary, as some of the pictures in this book show.

Unlike wearing seat-belts in cars, there is no mandatory requirement for either the driver or passengers to wear a lifejacket, and the decision becomes yours as the captain in charge of the vessel. Depending on the size of the boat, the weather, the age and experience of the crew, and the waters you are in, you may consider they are not needed.

In years gone by, a full lifejacket was cumbersome and bulky, and was often actually a hindrance, but the development of automatic self-inflating braces-style jackets means there is little reason for you not to wear them at all times, and our advice would be

Right and Below:
The modern inflatable lifejacket does not restrict your movements, and can be worn at all times

that you and your passengers always put them on.

But if you don't, as a minimum there should be one on board for every person likely to be on the boat, and everyone should be shown how to put them on before you cast off.

And you should also understand the differences between the types. A Lifejacket should have sufficient buoyancy to turn an unconscious person on their back, and keep their head above water. They are defined

by their buoyancy, and will be either 150 Newtons, suitable for most conditions, or 275 Newtons, for severe weather offshore. They are either inflatable, or part inflatable/foam. A Buoyancy Aid will keep you afloat if you are conscious, and help is close at hand, so are suitable for calm waters. They also come in two buoyancies, 100 Newtons, or 5 Newtons, and are always foam. Of course an inflatable type is no use for waterskiing, as you will set it off as soon as you get in the water!

Inflatable types should also be checked every year, and serviced if need be.

Chapter 5:
Finance & Insurance

So you have found your perfect boat, but now you need to find the money to buy it, then insure it. We guide you through the financial maze

Depending on the size and value of your boat, you may be able to buy it with cash, but in many cases you may need to pay all or some of the price with a loan.

Borrowing the money may enable you to buy a better or newer boat than you could otherwise afford, or to buy it sooner, or it may leave you with some spare cash to pay for extra equipment.

And while you should not look on your boat as an appreciating asset, equally it will not depreciate as fast as many other consumer goods, such as cars or computers, which means you will recover a sensible proportion of your outlay should you have to sell it at a later date.

There are several options available to raise a loan, and this chapter will help you choose the right one, but firstly you must decide how much you need to borrow, and how much you can afford to pay

back every month.

When assessing the size of the loan you need, do not just take the price of the boat. To this you should add the annual running costs. These will include mooring, if you are going to keep it in a marina, insurance, maintenance for engine and hull, fuel, plus necessary equipment such as lifejackets and waterproofs. Also always leave a contingency fund, to cover the unthought of and unbudgeted items which will inevitably crop up.

Then work out how much you can pay back every month. It may seem boring to total all your income and outgoings, but it is essential if your boat is not to become a financial burden.

What loans are on offer?

Once you have decided on the amount you want to borrow, and how much you can afford to pay, you need to look at the options available.

These will basically divide into secured and unsecured loans.

The overall payback rate can be expressed in a variety of often bewildering terms, but the one common denominator is APR, the Annual Percentage Rate. This is the overall interest you will have to pay on the loan per year, including all fees, and by law must be stated by the lender.

The simplest unsecured loan

is to use your Credit Card, and may be suitable for smaller craft up to £5,000. But you will be paying back at an APR of 16% or so. This means if you borrow £1,000, you will be paying £12.40 per month interest, but the original loan will still be unpaid.

Larger unsecured or personal loans are available from many sources today - banks, finance houses, building societies, even Tescos Provided you have a good credit record they will be quick and easy to set up, require no deposit, and can be paid back over five to ten years. The maximum loan available will be around £15-25,000.

APR on an unsecured loan at the moment will be in the region of 6-7%, though obviously this will vary all the time, depending on the base lending rate set by the Bank of England.

On a £10,000 loan over a five year period, this will give you a monthly repayment of around £195. Or looking at it the other way, at the end of five years you will have paid back £11,500.

The next option is a secured loan. The security for this will generally be your house, or the boat itself. If you already own a house, building societies or the major high street banks will advance you further secured loans whose maximum amount depends on the value of the house less the balance of your outstanding mortgage. Typically this may

Left: Make sure your motor insurance covers you for towing, and that the rig complies with all the regulations and laws. The boat insurance should cover it for damage or theft when on the road

Below: Make sure your insurance covers you for water-skiing and wake-boarding, and especially if you intend towing inflatable toys

give you a maximum amount of £40,000, with an APR close to that of the mortgage itself. Drawbacks are that there can be delays in setting them up, as well as fees for the service, plus penalties for early redemption.

Also you must remember that your house is being used as security against the loan, and as the small print in the adverts reminds us, it could be at risk if you fail to pay the instalments.

So the final option is what is termed a marine mortgage. This is a secured loan, that uses the boat itself as the security.

These are generally offered by specialist companies in the market, who deal extensively with loans for boats. Typically they will be available for sums greater than £25,000, and in theory up to any amount, depending on the value of the boat. They will usually be for a maximum of 80% of the value of the boat, meaning you have to find a 20% deposit, and will carry an arrangement fee, which will be around £450 for a £50,000 boat.

Repayment periods will generally be for ten years, but again longer may be available.

Advantages are that you will be dealing with specialists who are often boat owners themselves, and who will be

familiar with the problems of boat purchase and ownership. This will speed up the process of getting the loan, but even so there will be procedures involved.

For instance you will need a survey and valuation report, if the boat being bought is secondhand. Insurance will be mandatory, and certain restrictions on the use of the boat may be written into the contract - commonsense points such as a requirement to notify the lender of any change of home mooring over the period of the loan.

Depending on the finance house, registration of the boat may be required, to prove

ownership, though for craft up to £50,000 or so, normally moored in the UK it is likely to be waived. Part I registration under the 1995 Merchant Shipping Act costs £175-230.

As with all loans, the longer the period the mortgage is spread over, the smaller the monthly repayments will be, but the greater the total repaid will be. Recent options include interest-only payments, or balloon repayments, where you pay a low monthly rate, with the balance of the loan at the end of the period. Useful if you sell the boat, but remember its used value after 10 years may be only 50% of what it cost new.

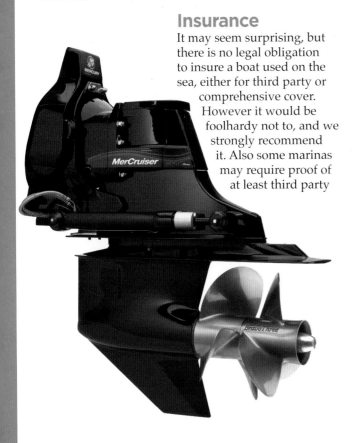

Insurance

It may seem surprising, but there is no legal obligation to insure a boat used on the sea, either for third party or comprehensive cover. However it would be foolhardy not to, and we strongly recommend it. Also some marinas may require proof of at least third party

Above:
Propellers, especially stainless ones are magnets for thieves. Fit a locking security nut such as the McGard shown here

Right:
Always fit an approved wheel-clamp and hitch-lock. In winter jack up the trailer and remove the other wheel, or fit a special clamp that replaces the wheel

insurance, and all inland waterways now require this.

Boat insurance is not expensive, a fact that reflects the basic safety of our sport, and how few claims are actually made. Premiums are nothing like what you pay for your car.

Obviously quotes will vary between companies, and for differing value boats with different circumstances, but approximate figures before no-claims bonus will be around £275 for a 5m RIB worth £15,000. Waterskiing cover will add another £25 or so. This will cover you for UK inland and coastal waters, up to 12 miles offshore. It should also give you up to 30 days use abroad, but you need to confirm this, and let them know when you are going.

As with all insurance it is essential that you give full and accurate details of the boat, where it is kept, where it will be used, and the experience of the owner or skipper. Equally important, you must inform the insurance company of any material changes in these details. Deciding whether a change is material or not can be difficult, but err on the safe side.

If you are towing the boat, you need to check with your car insurance that you are covered. Normally the boat insurance will cover the boat and trailer if they are stolen or damaged, but the car insurance will cover you if you cause third party damage. So if you back the boat into another car your motor insurance will cover the damage to that car, the boat insurance will cover the boat. However, it is vital that you comply with all legal requirements for the rig, or your motor insurance may decline liability. This includes complying with the weight restrictions on what your car can tow, and ensuring the tyres, brakes and lights are legal.

A boat on a trailer will have to be secured by an approved wheel-clamp or hitch-lock. Outboard motors must be secured with an approved lock in addition to their normal clamps. This is particularly important during winter, when the boat could be left unattended for long periods.

Trailer security tips

Here are a few tips for keeping you boat secure on its trailer.

Always fit an approved wheel-clamp or hitch lock. Even if you stop in a Motorway Service Station, fit a hitch-lock. During winter, jack the trailer up on blocks and remove the opposite wheel to the clamp. It is in any case a good idea to take the weight off the tyres and suspension if they are left for prolonged periods in one position. Caravan shops have a wide range, or go to

www.bulldogsecure.com.

For light boats that could be lifted off, put a strong motor-cycle cable lock through the bow eye and round a welded part of the trailer.

Secure the outboard with either a clamp lock, or better still a security nut on one of the through-transom bolts. Go to www.outboardmotorlocks.co.uk for a full range.

Propellers are magnets for thieves, especially shiny stainless steel ones, but you can buy security nuts similar to those on your car's alloy wheels. EP Barrus and Mariner/Mercury dealers sell the McGard range. www.barrus.co.uk, www.mcgard.com.

Remove all loose items, especially full fuel tanks, which are now worth more than their weight in gold. You shouldn't leave petrol over the winter anyway, as it goes stale and gums up the carburettors, so siphon it into your car.

LARSON

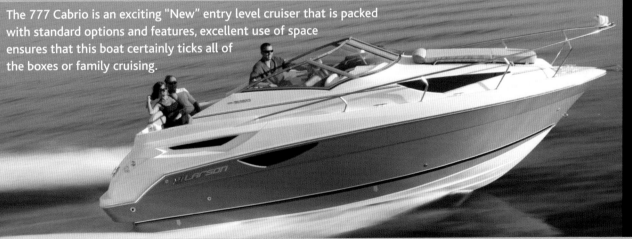

Chapter 6:
Electronics

Tim Bartlett guides you through the navigation and communication aids you will need on your sportsboat or RIB

Right: A fish-finder also shows you the depth of water under your boat, displaying a continuous line of the sea-bed as you travel over it

Below: A traditional compass is probably the most important first navigation aid on any boat. Simple, easy to read, it does not rely on batteries, electrics, or electronics to work, and together with a paper chart will enable you to find your way under any conditions

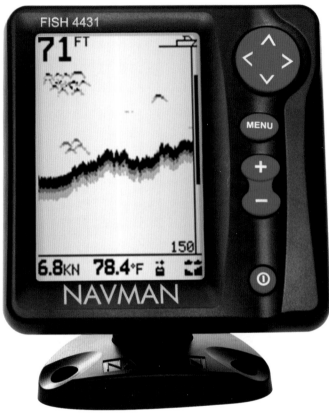

When you buy a car, you take it for granted that it will have a speedometer and fuel gauge, and any other necessary instruments. Today it will also often have its own built-in GPS navigation system.

But boats are different. A new boat may have nothing at all, or just the minimum, while a secondhand boat may have a hotchpotch of different bits of kit, fitted to suit the needs and budgets of several past owners. So before you set out to sea, you must make sure your craft has the essential instruments to keep tabs on the engine, and to navigate.

Compass

The minimum requirement for any boat, apart from one that is going to spend its entire life on enclosed waters, is a compass. This can be either traditional or electronic.

The traditional and still the simplest compass has changed little in principle from those used by Drake and Nelson, and consists of a magnetic disc, floating in a bowl of liquid. In their modern form they are usually in plastic domes, rather than flat-topped bowls, and are marked in degrees instead of the confusing old 'points' notation. But they don't wear out or go out of fashion, so a secondhand boat probably won't need a new compass. Do check, though, that the dome isn't cracked or cloudy, and that the liquid inside is clear and free of bubbles.

If you're buying a compass, pick one that is a reasonable size for the boat (at least 10mm of compass diameter for every metre of boat length). Choose one with built-in lighting and compensator magnets if you can, and make sure that it is suitable for where you intend to fit it - don't go for a mini-binnacle like the one in the photograph, for instance, if it is to be mounted on a near-vertical dashboard. Mount it away from any large metallic objects or wiring, and get it swung or checked against another unit periodically. You can use a handheld GPS to check it, but keep the two well apart.

Electronic compasses work on the fluxgate principle, and display your heading either as a circle on a screen, or just degrees. You can either buy a stand-alone version, or more likely will find one already incorporated in your chartplotter, or GPS.

Log & depth sounder

The other essential requirements are a log, or speedometer, for measuring speed and distance, and an echo sounder for measuring depth of water. Often these will be combined in one instrument.

The log can either work using a paddlewheel through the bottom of the boat, or a pitot head in your outboard leg. Both will give you your speed through the water. The other method of measuring speed is with a GPS, using more, their effect will be small, but at slower speeds they need to watched out for. Also if they are running across your direction of travel, they will have a marked effect as the distance you travel increases.

An echo sounder works by using a transducer in the bottom of the boat to send an ultrasonic signal to the seabed, and measuring the time it takes for the echoes to be returned. The longer the delay, the deeper the water. Fishfinders work in exactly the same way, except that they display the results as a graph or pictorial display, instead of numbers, and so can also pick up shoals of fish between the boat and the bottom. But more importantly they also give you a record of how the seabed is rising or falling.

The ideal sportsboat instrument is a combined fish-finder and log, complete with a transom-mount transducer for easy DIY installation. Budget versions of these can be found for around £150.

GPS

In-car navigation systems have really taken off over the past couple of years, but the Global Positioning System (GPS) on

which they depend has been around a lot longer, and small boats have been using it for at least twenty years.

A GPS receiver tells you where you are, usually within 10-15m. But early in their development, the manufacturers twigged that there were various other features that might be useful, such as how fast you are moving, in what direction, and how your position compares with where you want to go (a waypoint).

Simple, hand-held GPS sets start from less than £100, from suppliers such as Garmin, Magellan, and Lowrance. Any of them will tell you where you are, will store more waypoints than you need, and will do basic calculations such as working out your track and velocity, the range and bearing to any selected waypoint, and how far you have strayed off the straight line route between your starting point and the next waypoint -- known as your cross track error.

At that price they are well worth having, if only as a back-up to other systems. Do remember, though, that you'll also need a paper chart (map) in order to relate the latitude and longitude shown on its display to the real world around you.

Chart plotters

The next step forward is a chart-plotter. This takes position data from a GPS receiver (usually built in), and displays it on an electronic map on a screen. This enables you to see

atellite signals. This will ;ive you your speed over the ;round.

If you are traveling in a ake, or the sea with no tide unning, speed hrough the water nd speed over the ;round will be the ame. But if a tide is unning in the same lirection as your ravel, your speed ver the ground vill be greater than our speed through he water, and if t is against you, our speed will ,e reduced. Tides ;enerally run at ,etween one and wo knots, so in . fast sportsboat t say 20 knots or

Far left: A handheld GPS is a useful piece of equipment for finding where you are on the smallest boat, and will also give you your track, speed and course to steer.

Left: A chart plotter is a more sophisticated version of the same principal, but its screen not only carries a chart of where you are, it can also display a wide range of other information from your engine, radar, and depth sounder

Left: This simple fixed GPS shows speed, course and heading

Above: Chart plotters hold their data on removable cartridges, which can be updated and expanded to keep their information accurate

Below: Another Multi Function Display chart plotter

where you are going, which direction you are pointing in, your speed over the ground, and any drift caused by tides. It shows you the water and land around you, channels, buoys, harbours and obstructions, and the depth of the water. It may also have a fish-finder display that you can switch to, or show simultaneously.

There are dozens of models available, each with characteristics that make them particularly suitable for some people, and less suitable for others.

Screen size
Go for the biggest your dashboard and budget will allow. The bigger it is, the easier it will be to read as you are bouncing across the water.

To see why, take a piece of A4 paper, and fold it in half, to A5 size. That's roughly equivalent to a 10 inch (250mm) screen. Fold in half again, to the size of a postcard, and it's comparable with a 7 inch screen. Halving it yet again produces a 5 inch screen, and another halving -- to something rather smaller than a credit card -- yields the equivalent of a 3.6 inch screen.

Resolution
Resolution refers to the graininess of the screen image, and is usually measured in pixels -- the number of dots that make up the screen image. But it also depends on the size of the screen. A 15-inch computer monitor, for instance, running at the common 1024x768 resolution, is about 85 dots per inch --

almost exactly the same as a 7-inch screen with a resolution of 480x320. 100 pixels per inch is generally suitable for your use.

Cartography
Most chart plotters include a base map, but realistically this needs to be improved by using an added electronic chart. Detailed marine charts are available in the form of cartridges, similar to the memory cards used in digital cameras. Unfortunately, most makes of plotter are tied to one type of cartography, as well as to a particular type of cartridge, so your choice of cartography has a big bearing on the plotter you choose.

C-Map Max, Garmin Bluechart G2, and Navionics Platinum could all be called latest generation electronic charts: they include aerial and satellite photographs, can create 3-D images of the shape of the seabed, and include details of tides and currents.

C-Map NT, Garmin Bluechart and Navionics Gold could be seen as the older generation: they lack some of the bells and whistles of their later counterparts, but generally offer more coverage for less outlay.

Paper Charts
If your electronics should fail, you will be completely lost, so you should always carry an up-to-date paper chart for the area you are cruising in. Keep it in a waterproof bag, or buy the waterproof versions. A paper chart also allows you to plan your route at home, and gives a greater overview of where you are going.

Radar
Plotter manufacturers are gradually moving away from calling their products plotters. The word now is MFD. The initials stand for Multi Function Display, and reflect the fact that using a large colour display for just one purpose is a waste. So plotters are increasingly designed to accept and display information from various other sensors, including fish finders and engine instruments and

Left: Broadband radar has low power emissions, so can be mounted low down on a RIB mast, without causing any risk to the occupants of the boat

increasingly radar.

To professional seafarers, radar is an almost indispensable tool, ranking way above GPS and chart plotters. But for sportsboats, it's a would-be-nice rather than a must-have. It's great for pilotage in poor visibility, and unbeatable as a collision avoidance tool in fog. But until recently the performance of very small radar scanners has been disappointing. And they have had to be mounted on tall masts so their radiation does not harm the crew.

But all this has changed with the development of Broadband Radar. This gives enhanced picture quality from a small scanner, has low power requirements, and most importantly its low power outputs do not harm humans, so the scanner can be

mounted low down on the A-frame of a RIB for instance.

Communication
Just as electronic charts are taking over from paper, so radio long ago took over from

flares, flags, and lamps as the primary method of calling for help. And, unlike a box of flares, a radio isn't a piece of emergency equipment that you hope you're never going to use - it's for ordinary, everyday communications, such as booking a marina berth or arranging a rendezvous, just as much as for distress situations.

There are many different types of radio communications, but for sportsboats Marine VHF is by far the most important. But even when you've narrowed the choice down that far, there is still a lot to choose from.

The most basic choice is whether you want a fixed radio or a portable set.

Portable equipment always seems inherently appealing, and in the case of VHF radios that appeal is boosted by the fact that portables are usually cheaper than their fixed-mount

Left: Many hand-held VHF radios today will float if you drop them overboard

Bottom Left: A fixed VHF will have greater power output and hence greater range than a handheld version

Below and Right: An EPIRB, Emergency Position Indicating Radio Beacon, will signal your position to rescue services via satellites.

VHF Radio and the Law

To use marine VHF — even a hand-held — you need two different kinds of licence.

The first is either a Ship Radio Licence or a Ship Portable Radio Licence. It's free, but if you don't get one, Ofcom might recoup some of the costs of issuing them to other people by imposing an on-the-spot fine on you! (www.ofcom.org.uk/licensing/olc/) **The second** is an "Authority to operate". It's like a driving licence, in that it relates to an individual, rather than to a particular boat or radio, and that it lasts (in theory) for life. Get it either by taking a short exam or (much better) by doing a one-day course. **The total fee for a course and certificate is usually about £100:**

Contact the RYA for details: (www.rya.org.uk/Courses/specialistshortcourses.htm)

counterparts. A portable can be taken off the boat, to stop it being stolen, or you can take it with you if you go on someone else's boat, but with a price to pay in terms of performance.

Compared with a fixed radio, whose output is 25 watts, the fact that a portable has to run off an internal rechargeable battery limits its power to about 5 watts, and limits the time of use before having to recharge it to 6-10 hours, while the need for a short, flexible aerial makes it less efficient at both transmitting and receiving. The result is that a pair of hand-helds are doing well if they can communicate with each other over a range of three or four miles, or 10-12 miles to a coast radio station such as the coastguard. By contrast, a 25-watt fixed set with a good aerial, properly installed so that it is vertical (rather than leaning backwards) may well manage ten miles from boat to boat, and forty miles to a coast radio station such as the coastguard.

Fixed radios are slightly more expensive to buy, and you need to add the cost of an aerial (at least £30, for a decent one). Fitting it is an easy DIY job, but if you choose to get someone else to do it, of course it will add to the cost.

First, though, there's another decision to be made: do you want a DSC radio or not? The initials stand for Digital Selective Calling, and refer to a semi-automatic system that makes establishing communication with another

vessel almost like making a call on a mobile phone. You choose the vessel you want to talk to, either from a built in 'phone book' or by dialling in a nine-digit number, and you choose the channel (frequency) you want to talk to. Then you press the go button, and wait for a reply! If you get into trouble, the same system allows you to send an automated distress message at the push of a button. The overwhelming majority of fixed VHF radios have DSC controllers built in. Combined units sell in such huge numbers that you can pick up a perfectly serviceable DSC radio for less than £100.

Mobile phones
These have now become so universal that the Coastguard are accepting their value as emergency communication aids. Keep yours dry, in a waterproof bag, or purpose-made waterproof pouch, or an inside jacket pocket. Do not keep it in your trouser pocket, as it will quickly get wet with spray or rain. Get a car charger lead for it, and plug it into your boats 12V socket to keep it charged up.

EPIRBs
There's one other piece of communication equipment that the more adventurous sports boater might want to consider, and that's an EPIRB.

The initials stand for Emergency Position Indicating Radio Beacon, but it's really an automated satellite communications terminal that is only about the size of a pint glass, but in the event of an emergency is capable

of transmitting a distress signal to any of several satellites orbiting a few hundred kilometres above the Earth. The satellite then works out where the signal is coming from, and sends the information back down to Search and Rescue Authorities around the world.

Each EPIRB also transmits a lower-frequency homing signal for lifeboats or helicopters, and most have a flashing light that will guide rescuers to its exact spot.

Prices, for basic EPIRBs, start at about £300. For about £200 more there are alternative versions that have built-in GPS receivers that enable them to include position in the initial distress message.

aking time out on one of Salcombe's beautiful beaches

CHAPTER 7:
Training

As with any sport, learning how to do it before you take your first steps afloat alone is essential, not only to get the most enjoyment from your boating, but more importantly for the safety of everyone aboard, and other boats around you. John Mendez describes what you will be taught in the various courses.

Many people assume that handling a boat is just like driving a car and so if they can drive a car what can be difficult about a boat? But nothing could be further from the truth. Yes it has an engine, wheel and throttle, but everything else is completely different.

Many countries actually make some sort of training compulsory before you can go afloat, but the UK still has a voluntary system, which still enables you to achieve the necessary standard, but in a less pressured and more enjoyable way.

In the UK training courses are run primarily by training centres either recognised by the RYA (Royal Yachting Association) www.rya.org.uk, who cater for all water users, or by more specialised groups such as BSAC (British Sub Aqua Club) for those who are primarily interested in diving, or by BWS (British Water Ski) for the skiers amongst you. All the standard courses have similar content but with additions for diving or water-skiing where appropriate. The specialist providers have higher levels for their own disciplines but only the RYA courses offer a progression to the higher levels of navigation and night work for general boating.

The most useful course for

Above: Explaining the engine instruments

Course content

All courses start with some basic safety topics and then aim to spend as much time on the water as possible to give basic understanding and confidence afloat. The syllabus covers:

- Launching and recovery
- Safety equipment, emergency procedures and the 'Kill Cord'
- Engine checks
- Types of craft and how they differ
- Confined space manoeuvring
- Mooring
- Man overboard procedure
- Anchoring
- Towing
- High speed handling
- Collision regulations
- Buoyage
- Basic chartwork and navigation
- Tides
- Communication afloat

When you have gained some basic experience then you can move on and try an Intermediate Course. This includes daylight passage planning and good use of electronics afloat, or an Advanced Course which includes faster passage work, how to deal with rougher conditions and some night-time passage experience. The RYA have also introduced a two-day basic navigation course especially for people with smaller craft to allow them to learn the basics of navigation to help them keep safe afloat.

Also essential and also a legal requirement if you have a VHF radio, whether hand-held or fixed is the one-day course in maritime radio, again this is run by the RYA. You will also need to obtain a licence for the VHF equipment that you own. This is now free to obtain from OFCOM.

First steps

Whether you decide to do a formal training course or just try and learn from books and experienced friends, there are several things to consider before you take your first steps afloat.

Safety equipment is essential on the boat, but what you need has to balanced against the area that you are going to be boating in. A lake or river won't require as much equipment as if you are going to sea in a sheltered bay, however a trip across a large bay or around a headland will require more again. The essentials can be split into two groups, personal equipment and items for the boat.

the beginner or even someone who has been afloat before but is rusty, is the RYA National Powerboat Certificate – Level 2. This is similar to the BSAC Boat Handling Course or the BWS Ski Boat Driver Award.

Courses usually take two days and cover theory as well as practical handling. They are usually carried out in the school's boat, but can sometimes be arranged on your own craft.

And by the way, don't just think that training should be for one driver on the boat. Partners and children should be included if they are going to be regular crew, as it gives them greater confidence and enjoyment of the boating experience, and more importantly will enable them to take over if the driver falls ill - or falls overboard!

Training schools advertise in the boating magazines, or a list of them can be obtained from the RYA. Alternatively many boat dealers will put you in touch with ones that they have experience of.

It is important to wear a lifejacket or buoyancy aid that is suitable for the boating and waters you are going to be in, and to understand what you have on and how it works. A life-jacket is designed to turn an unconscious casualty the correct way up, with the automatic types inflating immediately you hit the water. However this would be no use at all for water skiing as it will inflate immediately – in this case a buoyancy aid would be more appropriate as it provides a degree of buoyancy for a person who can swim.

Below: Here is just some of the safety equipment you should carry aboard. The rest is described in the text. Make sure you know where it is, and it is all in working order

Personal equipment will change with the seasons and how far you are going, but will comprises a minimum of: Lifejacket/buoyancy aid for everybody aboard, plus spares for any guests you may take with you, waterproofs, dry-suit or even a wetsuit, and then, depending on the time of year possibly gloves, hat, boots, sun cream, sunglasses, food, water or drinks.

Boat equipment will also vary greatly with area, however a minimum of equipment that you will need to add to a 'bare boat' would comprise an anchor with warp, paddles, lines, fenders, flares for the area, a VHF radio, GPS, Compass, First Aid kit, sharp knife, tool kit, fire extinguisher, charts and a spare kill cord. Other items can be considered as you gain experience and go further a field.

Launching
The next step you will have to understand is launching the boat. This can be either traumatic or straightforward, depending on how well you have practised and prepared, but for any trailable boat it enables you to keep your craft at home, saving mooring charges, and allows you to travel to different waters, and even abroad.

If you have never launched a boat before, don't make your first attempt on a busy summer weekend, with all the family waiting to go out on the water. Instead choose a quiet weekday evening, with just a friend, and no-one watching. Here you can practice the techniques in peace.

Even when you know what you are doing, it is essential to be prepared, and take things at a steady pace, without rushing. Boats are heavy items and you don't want to injure yourself or anyone else. The best approach is to arrive early with a plan of action. The first step will be to park up away from the slipway and let the trailer bearings cool down before you dunk them in salty water. If you are more than an hour's drive to the launch site this can easily take a good 20 minutes, but this time is not wasted as there is lots to do. Preparation is key here, as you want to be on the slipway itself for the minimum amount of time. This is not only courteous to other users, it avoids a queue of impatient people building up.

Much of this preparation can be done before you leave home, especially if it's a slipway that you have not used before. Check who it belongs to? Is it a public slip, or a club's and who administers it? Do you have to pay? If so, to whom, how much and where do you find them on the day? Some slipways need an annual licence. Some local council-owned slips are asking these days to see your insurance before they will give permission to launch, and some slips which specialise in personal watercraft are asking you to have your RYA licence first. Boat Launch www.boatlaunch.co.uk provides good basic information and phone numbers so you can make your plans in advance. Obviously check the weather and tides to see if they are suitable on the day of your intended trip and remember that neap tides will always give less tidal range and hence less flow to contend with than springs. Lastly, can the slipway be used at all states of the tide, or just a couple of hours either side of high water? Or do you have the situation where you can launch at one slip and recover at another locally?

Here is a basic checklist we use before we launch, that you can tailor to your own craft:

- Inspect the boat to ensure no damage has occurred on route

- Put the drain plug in the boat - everyone forgets that once!

- Remove all the tie-down straps but not the winch-strap

- Remove the trailer board – its electrics don't like getting wet

- Keeping the winch strap attached to the boat and making sure that the ratchet is locked, take the bow line round the winch post so that the boat can be released from on board the craft

- Put all your day's boating essentials aboard, secured so they don't slide when the boat goes down the slip

- Don't forget the ignition keys... and the kill cord

- Carry out your engine checks

- Turn the battery on and prime the fuel line

- Double check the safety equipment - if you have new boaters with you, this is the ideal time to show them this kit whilst they are concentrating properly on dry land.

- Make sure that everybody understands that they do not stand behind the boat and trailer on the slipway.

- Re-check the drain plug.......

When these preparations have been completed, you need to check the slipway self. Before you reverse nto it, walk over and inspect . Just ask yourself some imple questions:

Is it as steep as you need?

It is clean, or slippery and covered in weed?

Has a recent storm left a load of shingle on it?

Is it in good condition especially where the tow vehicle's wheels will be?

Are there any warning signs showing a drop off at the end?

Will you be able to reverse down with the trailer and tow vehicle together or will you need to use a rope between them to give enough depth of water for the boat to float off?

Ideally you need a minimum f two people to launch a boat one to drive the car and one o reverse the boat off. It can e done single-handed but it is arder work and needs more ractice.

Position the tow car and boat t the top of the slipway, make bsolutely sure that there is no-ne below you on the slipway, nen reverse the rig down until ou are just at the water's edge. Iake sure that the boat is now eld on by the bow line looped nder the winch post and ttached on board. Now release ne winch strap from the eye on the bow and get in. Ideally you now want to reverse the boat in, getting it just deep enough to allow you partially lower the engine and start it, letting it warm up briefly. Check forward and reverse gears. If all is well you can signal the car driver to reverse a touch more and as the boat is ready to float off you can come forward to release the bow line, move back to the helm, put the kill cord on and reverse away.

Basic checks

So having got your boat afloat and equipped, next we have to consider how does it actually drive.

Before you set off you will need to do basic engine checks and ensure that you have enough fuel.

Engine checks will depend upon what type of motor you have but will usually comprise checking the oil level, drive belts and cooling water on an inboard, plus electrical connections and the fuel gauge. On an outboard it will include checking the oil, either in the sump of a four-stroke, or reservoir of a two-stroke, priming the fuel with the priming bulb, unscrewing the fuel-tank vent cap, and checking the propeller for any nicks and damage. Lastly check that the steering turns smoothly from hard over port to hard over starboard, and that the gears engage smoothly with

no drag or crunching. Once the engine has started you should check that the cooling water is coming out of the outlet.

Your boat's controls are usually grouped around the helm. The most basic will have a wheel and a single-lever combined gear and throttle control. The wheel is turned to give steering and the gear lever/throttle allows you to engage either ahead or astern by releasing the interlock and then pushing to the first click position, either forward for ahead or backward for astern. It also allows you to push or pull it further in each direction to make the engine and boat increase speed in each direction by opening the throttle. The kill cord is usually located next to the ignition switch. When it is removed, the engine stops.

Left: You will be shown how to put your lifejacket on correctly

Left: Explaining the parts of the outboard and how they work

Chapter 7:
Training

In the UK training courses are run primarily by training centres either recognised by

BSAC - British Sub Aqua Club
www.bsac.com

BWS - British Waterski & Wakeboard
www.britishwaterski andwakeboard.org.uk

RYA - Royal Yachting Association
www.rya.org.uk

Therefore you should attach it to yourself, either round your wrist, or clipped to your belt, at all times the engine is running. If you should be thrown overboard, or fall down inside the boat, it will stop the engine. It is there for your's and every other water user's safety, wear it at all times afloat and check that it works each time you use the boat.

Handling

Handling your boat is governed by several factors. Understanding them and using them to your advantage allows all your boat trips to be much easier. The key points are: How windy is the day and how will this affect the boat. Is there any tidal stream? How heavy is the boat, as this affects its momentum? Where does it pivot in ahead and astern? How is it steered - outboard, outdrive, shaft and rudder?

When you consider these factors and look at your own particular craft, a picture begins to emerge of what to expect, before we have even set off.

Windage - A boat's windage is governed by how high and slab sided it is. A rib is much less affected than a small cruiser. Remembering how windy it is and where it is coming from is essential, especially in the marina.

Stream - the tidal stream affects all boats, but a high-sided sports boat may be more affected by wind than by stream.

Momentum - Carrying way and stopping. Unfortunately boats don't have brakes so you need to learn to use neutral, and if necessary reverse, to bring it to a halt. Good boat drivers spend a lot of time in neutral just letting the vessel move under its own momentum. Sometimes you may need to use a small amount of engine power to halt the last of this momentum; however it is best to make as much use of nature's brakes - the wind and stream.

Pivot Points

Unlike a car, which steers via its front wheels, a boat is steered by its rudder, or outboard, at the stern. Because of this, when you put the wheel over one way, the stern swings out the other way, while the bow only slowly follows the wheel. The pivot point for the turn on most boats is roughly one third of the way back from the bow, so the stern moves twice as fast as the bow. When going astern the pivot point moves aft and again with the wheel hard over to port (left) with astern gear engaged roughly the stern third of the vessel moves to port while the bow moves to starboard.

All boats pivot at slightly different points, and knowing where this is on your boat is one of the most important factors in all boat handling exercises.

How it steers

When the engine is put into ahead gear and the propeller turns, it provides forward thrust. But because of its rotation it also tries to move the stern to one side due to the paddle-wheel or prop effect. This affects shaft-drive boats more than outboards or sterndrives, while in duoprops it is non-existent. Shaft-drive boats are generally steered by rudders, which work by deflecting water passing over them. Because it is behind the propeller the effect is much greater when the propeller is turning. At slow speeds a burst of power is very effective as it dramatically increases the water flow over the rudder without increasing speed too much.

Outboards and sterndrives do not have rudders. Instead they steer by thrusting the water in the direction that the drive is turned.

Right: Planning your approach to a pontoon is essential

Left: Before casting off
make sure everyone
knows the sequence
for letting go the lines

But in both cases you only
get steering effect when the
prop is turning, hence the
phrase that you should mutter
to yourself every time you are
manoeuvring: **no gear - no
steer.**

Because you want the boat
to react immediately power
is applied it is best to turn the
wheel before going into gear.
This can easily be remembered
as: **wheel before gear.**

Because of the combination
of windage, stream, and its
handling characteristics, a
boat is often travelling as the
resultant of all of these effects.
Especially at slower speeds
is important to realise that
the boat is often not moving
in the direction it is pointing.
Learning how to read these
elements and use them to your
advantage is one of the key
factors in stress-free boating.

Because a boat steers better
when it has some forward
movement through the water,
is always best if possible to
carry out your manoeuvres
facing into any wind or stream.
Thus you are able to maintain
steerage way, while actually
staying in one position relative
to the ground, or use the
stream to kill your approach

speed without having to use
reverse.

Practice

Having grasped the basics of
how your boat handles, the
next step is to practise in an
area where you won't do any
damage if you get it wrong.
An open expanse of water, but
with a fixed object that can act
as a reference point is ideal. If
you can find a mooring buoy
to work around, that is even
better, provided there are no
other boats nearby.

Here you can practice the
theory that approaching into
the wind and stream gives
much greater control, that the
boat will respond perfectly to a
click of gear rather than burst
of power, and that plenty of
neutral and being patient pays
dividends.

However it is also essential
to always consider your escape
plan if you get it wrong, and
never be afraid to go round
again, rather than being forced
into a bad situation.

Coming alongside

When you have safely
mastered these techniques,
you can move onto a long,
unoccupied pontoon for some

gentle berthing practice, and
from here to a marina. The
general idea at all times is
to keep it as slow as you can
and always plan your escape
route. Sudden noisy bursts of
reverse power will unsettle
your passengers, tip your crew
member at the bow into the
water, and alert any casual
onlookers that a drama worth
watching is developing.

First line up yourself for your
initial approach, remembering
wherever possible to head
into the wind or stream,
whichever is giving the most
natural braking effect. Your
angle of approach should be
roughly 30° to the pontoon.
Gently approach using neutral
to control your speed. As
you get closer try to use the
boat's momentum to carry you
the last part and hopefully
the wind and stream will be
providing nature's brakes. If
you need a click of astern to
remove the last of the way,
that's fine. With practice you
can improve the manoeuvre
by turning the wheel towards
the pontoon at the last moment
and using a click of astern. This
has the effect of slowing the
boat, together with pulling it in
alongside.

John Mendez runs
Mendez Marine,
Swanwick,
an RYA-approved
Training School,
offering a full
range of powerboat
training courses

Chapter 8:

Above: Your first trip is the one you will remember the longest, so make sure it goes well, and you are fully prepared, with everyone safely aboard, and wearing their lifejackets

Chapter 8:
Your First Trip

Having reached the point where you have mastered how to launch your boat and control it at slow speeds, you are ready for your first trip. There are several factors to consider before you set off

In its simplest form a passage could be just a journey between two points, such as the slipway and a nearby beach. They may well even be in sight of each other and hence the journey could look relatively easy. However even a short journey can still have its problems, for instance without a chart how can you be certain that there is deep enough water between the two points chosen? Just because the sea looks wet does not mean that there is sufficient depth for your boat, especially as round the coasts of this country the tide can make the water level rise and fall by at least 16ft (5m) every six hours, and in some places as much as a massive 45ft (14m).

A chart gives you information on how much minimum depth there is at low water, and with a set of tide tables you can work out how deep it will be when you are traveling over that spot. There may be enough depth on your outbound journey in the morning, but not enough when you return in the afternoon. The chart will also give you the location of rocks and other obstructions that could bring you to grief.

Traditionally mariners used a compass to allow them to steer a straight course,

nowadays also use a GPS or satnav, possibly even with a small plotter screen to make things even easier. A GPS gives you your position by taking a signal from three satellites, the same as in your car satnav. It also allows you to set a course to steer between two points, but it does not know if the course you have chosen to steer is a safe one, if there is enough depth of water, or any obstructions. For this you need to have a paper chart, or a chart plotter, which gives you the same information on a screen. In fact the best arrangement is to use a combination of the two. A paper chart is easiest for planning your passage when you are at home, or ashore, but when you are afloat in a moving small boat, a plotter is easier to read and use. Though you should still take the chart along in a waterproof bag, in case the electronics fail.

Weather

For all boats the weather is often the deciding factor in deciding if you go or where you go, but this is especially true for a relatively small craft such as a sportsboat or RIB. And even if the boat may be capable of handling the conditions you encounter, your passengers or crew may not. Nothing destroys your future boating faster than frightening

the family on their first trip. And even if they are not aware of what the conditions could be like on the journey, it is up to you to make the right prediction, and make the decision to stay in port, or make a shorter passage in a sheltered direction. Making the decision to turn upstream for a pleasant afternoon potter rather than out to sea for a wet and bouncy ride is the mark of a mature skipper at any time, but particularly on your first trip.

Rather than relying on just the forecast for the day you have chosen, look at the forecasts in the period leading up to your day so that you can learn how the weather systems are moving and how they may change while you are out. The internet now has some really good sites for following the usual depressions that come over the UK, and with a bit of practice you can learn to make your own view of the days ahead. Then you can assess if it is a settled period or likely to be changeable.

And remember it is a combination of the wind strength, its direction, and the state of the tide that govern how large the waves are going to be. The longer the fetch, or the distance the wind has blown over open water, the bigger the waves are going to be. Therefore if the wind is coming off the land, the closer

aving made allowance for ny possible sideways drift aused by the tidal current, and his still works perfectly well oday. However many people

Left: Plan your route in advance, and make sure everyone aboard knows what it is. You can use a chart-plotter when you are underway, and you should enter the waypoints at home, or before you set out, but a paper chart is the best way to make your initial decisions, as you can see a wider view, and also use it at home, and then bring it with you

Above: Always be prepared to change your plans during the trip if the weather should deteriorate, and turn inshore or inland for a quiet potter, rather than an uncomfortable ride at sea

Right: Some of the equipment you will need to carry with you, plus of course lifejackets for everyone aboard

inshore you are, the smaller the waves, though obviously the shallower the water will be. The longer it has been blowing, the bigger the waves will be. And finally its direction relative to the tidal stream at any time is critical. If the wind is blowing in the same direction as the tide, the waves will be longer and less severe. If it is blowing against the direction of the tide, the shorter and steeper they will be - the classic wind-over-tide situation that mariners have feared through the ages.

The speed you will be able to keep up comfortably in your planing boat will be completely dependent on the size and steepness of the waves.

Plan B

With all this planning and preparation you will ideally have a great day, however, as we have said it is always best to have a plan B just in case!

Remember that your plan to go further and your perception of what is fun may be very different to rest of the crew, or even to just one person aboard, and that will spoil the trip for everyone. Even where they are

sitting on board can make a difference. For the helmsman, sitting up high, with the wheel to hang on to, and able to see the waves coming, a fast run across turbulent water can be exhilarating. But for the passengers behind, just a few inches from the screaming engine, and being thrown from side to side it can be a very different perspective.

It may be something simple like having an alternative port

that's not so far if the sea turns out choppier than expected, or just having a gentle potter rather than the intended fast run. Remember you don't have to go - there will always be another day - or you can offer the less brave an afternoon on the beach while the tough guys frighten themselves out at sea. You are in charge, and you must make the decisions - don't wait for the others to speak up

The engine

The modern marine engine is very reliable, as long as you keep it serviced and supply it with clean fuel, but just in case yours does falter or stop, do you have even the basic knowledge of what you can do? Carrying a simple tool kit together with a set of basic spares could easily fix some problems.

If you are not mechanically inclined then join one of the organisations that provide assistance at sea, or better still go and learn about your engine - what you can and can't do. Also remember that if your engine should stop, you can always anchor. This can stop a minor breakdown becoming a major problem if you drift into dangerous waters, and also gives time for you to sort it out. At the same time, by holding the boat's head into waves, the anchor can make the motion on board easier, allowing you to work on the engine. However if repair is beyond your abilities then the Coastguard would rather you called them early and advise them of the situation so they can organise assistance.

The Passage

The key here is don't be too ambitious on your first trip. It's all too easy to set off on the great adventure which ends up going wrong, so start with something simple. It may just be a trip across the bay, and even better taking along a more experienced friend. Or teaming up with another boat similar to yours, whose crew is more experienced. Or you could join a club so that they are several of you going - being with others can really help your confidence and there is the added benefit that help is at hand.

Being prepared is the most important thing. You will need to have the correct charts for the area, and have worked out your route beforehand. If you have a GPS or plotter you should have entered the waypoints at home in the days leading up to your trip. You should check alternative bolt-holes if they should prove necessary. Are there other harbours or slipways on the

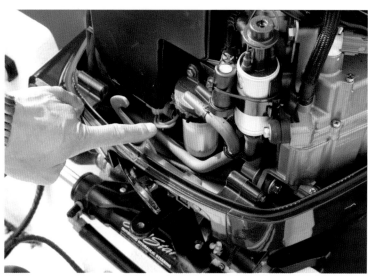

Left: The minimum navigation electronics area depth sounder and chart-plotter, either separate or combined

Above: If possible choose a slipway with convenient pontoons alongside, so you can get everyone on board safely, and do not have to set off in a rush

Opposite Page: Now you are ready for your first voyage

▪▪▪ ▬▬▬▬▬

route that you can divert to if necessary, and do they have water at all states of the tide on your chosen day?

As we have said the weather is the main factor which governs your day. You can check the forecast in advance, but double-check on the day that all is as expected and do remember that it can still change! Boat wise you will probably have checked all the kit many times, but it's the little things that can catch you out - when did you last charge the handheld VHF or buy spare batteries for the GPS? And now that you are going a bit further you will need to add in spare fuel, food and drinks and **remember the golden rule:**

Before the big day, if you are towing the boat to the coast, check that the trailer, lighting board, tyres, brakes and bearings have been serviced and are functioning correctly. Don't leave this to the morning of the trip. Choose an easy launch site or one you have been to before, preferably with good pontoons alongside so you can get everyone on board easily and safely. Double check

the tide to make sure that you can launch and recover easily. If its only available for a short period either side of high water that can easily add to the pressure. Go through the checklist we drew up in the previous chapter.

When you are launched and have got all the crew on board, lifejackets and kill cord on and you are ready to cast off, just pause for a moment and have a quick double-check – and most importantly show the other people on board how to use the controls, start and stop the engine, raise a Mayday by VHF, and know where you hid the flares and the first aid kit.

The Golden Rule
▪ Tell someone where you are going
▪ How many are in your group
▪ When you intend to be back
▪ And lastly and perhaps most importantly, how they should raise the alarm if you don't return at the intended time.

Chapter 9:
Waterskiing & Wakeboarding

Towing a waterskier, wakeboarder or inflatable toy behind your boat can be great fun, but it must be safe. We give you the essential tips

Once you have mastered your boat handling, got your first trips under your belt, and found your favourite beach or cove, it won't be long before some of the crew members, usually the younger ones start asking what else they can do behind the boat.

For many years the only option was waterskiing, but today there is a huge variety of things you can tow, including single or twin skis, wakeboards, which have largely taken over for recreational use, knee-boards, discs, and every size and shape of inflatable toy. These require varying degrees of skill, and

all provide huge fun for those who like getting wet, but they must be treated with great care if you are not to have accidents. It is not just a case of tying something to the transom then opening the throttle. You must prepare your boat and its crew carefully beforehand.

The engine

The first question is what is your boat capable of towing in the first place. The extra drag behind may prove too much for your engine, and the loads put on the structure may overload the hull, or make it dangerous to handle.

As you will have already discovered, when you open the throttle it takes a certain time

before the boat gets up on the plane. The amount of time is dependent on various factors, including the size of the engine, the propeller fitted, how it is trimmed, and the number

Below: Purpose-designed wake-board boats will have a tower to stow the boards on, and keep the tow-line high.

Right: Dual-purpose boats will have the tower, plus a cuddy cabin forward

of passengers on board, and where they are sitting.

Obviously the more horsepower, the faster you will plane, so if you are expecting to be doing a lot of watersports, go for the larger option when you are buying. But even the same engine will perform differently depending on the pitch of the propeller fitted. A finer pitch prop will give more thrust, and get you on the plane faster, but at the expense of some top speed. If there is a choice of propellers, go for the finer option if you are going to be towing a lot, or even consider having two props.

Your engine will almost certainly have power trim, and you should learn how to use this. For the fastest initial take-off you should trim the leg right in, but then be ready to trim out as you come onto

Left: Inflatable toys can be great fun for everyone, but you still need to handle them carefully

Above: This 4.5m RIB with 50hp will pull a light-weight wakeboarder. You must always have at least two people in the tow-boat, with one driving, looking forward, and one observer watching the skier. If the third person sits up in the bow, it helps the boat get on the plane quicker

the plane. Practice this many times without someone behind, so it becomes second nature. You don't want to get up to top speed with the leg trimmed in, as it will force the bow down and make the boat difficult to steer.

The more passengers aboard, the slower the boat will be to plane, but you can use these to your advantage by getting someone to sit right up in the bow. This will get you on the plane faster, but should only be done in relatively calm conditions, as they will be bounced around in waves. In theory they can make their way back aft once you are planing, but again this should be done cautiously.

The weight of the person being towed, and what they are on makes a huge difference. Waterskis require the most

power to get them up out of the water, with a mono-ski being even harder. They also require much more skill and practice to use. Wake-boards are much easier to pull, with their wide planing area and inherent buoyancy offering less drag, and are much easier to get the hang of.

Inflatable toys are the easiest to pull, and easiest for the people on them, but they still require great care in their use.

The boat

Your boat must be stable enough to withstand the loads of someone swinging from side to side behind it. You need a minimum 4m RIB with 40hp to tow a light person on a wake-board or inflatable, preferably 4.5m with 50hp. As the weight of the person increases, the loads go up correspondingly,

and for safety you need a large boat.

It must have a strongly-attached towing point. Purpose-designed ski-tow boats have a substantial ski-pole, mounted in the centre of the boat, well forward of the transom. This reduces the effect on the steering as the skier swings left and right. It is also high enough that the tow-rope passes well above the transom.

Your new RIB or sportsboat may have the option of a removable ski-pole, with an area of the hull strengthened to take it. Choose this if you are going to be doing a lot of serious towing. Or it may have a ski-hook, mounted forward of the engine.

Failing that you will have to use the transom hooks. These are fitted partly to enable the boat to be secured on the

railer, and partly for towing skiers. The downside is that as the skier swings either side, they pull the stern of the boat that way, requiring greater concentration from the driver. You also need to make up a bridle at the end of the tow-line, so the pull is central.

The tow-line should be polypropylene, as this floats and so is less likely to get dragged into the prop. It should also be brightly-coloured, so you can see it at all times. Purpose-designed ski-lines combine all of these.

The skier

The person being towed must be aware that they are going to get wet, thrown around, and dragged through the water. This may seem obvious, but it still comes as a surprise the first time it happens to you. It may seem very graceful when you watch a skilled skier, but the first time you take a nose-dive at 20 knots is a major shock to the system.

Unless it is a very hot day in summer, when the water is warm, and you are only playing for a few minutes, they should be wearing a wet-suit. Again it can quickly get unpleasant and cold.

It goes without saying that they should be wearing a life-jacket, but again the correct design is essential. Preferably it should be a purpose-designed ski vest. This will be less restricting, but it will be snug-fitting, with extra straps to keep it from riding up.

For complete safety, when there are several riders on inflatables, they should wear protective helmets, as they can bang heads with the other riders. Again your dealer will be able to supply the correct ones.

The Crew

"It takes three to ski" is the motto of all skiers, and it is essential that you follow this rule. As well as the person being towed, you have must one person driving the boat, concentrating only on what is ahead, while a responsible observer sits in a rear-facing seat, always watching the skier, and relaying instructions to the driver. If the skier should fall off, the observer must watch their position in the water at all times, and guide the driver safely back to them.

Never have just one person in the boat, and never break this rule.

It is preferable that at least one of the three people has some experience, either from being with other users, or they can undergo specific training. The British Waterski & Wakeboard Federation, www.bwsf.co.uk, have a set training syllabus, which is undergoing revision at this moment, and they will provide you with a list of approved training schools. This will have three levels, Observer, Driver, and Advanced Driver. This will result in three Ski Boat Driver Awards, SBDA 1, 2 &3.

They recommend that any ski-boat driver should have an SBDA, and some water or harbour authorities may make this a requirement.

They have also developed a Code of Safety Recommendations, aimed at ensuring that watersports of all kinds can be enjoyed safely without danger to the participants or to other water users. This can be downloaded from their website, and contains invaluable information.

This includes suggested hand signals to be used between skier and observer, essential for clear and safe communication.

For the driver it includes the instruction that you should never put the engine in reverse when a skier is in the water behind the boat, and you should also switch the engine off when you are letting the skier over the side, or bringing them back aboard. When turning back to a fallen skier, you should always keep them on the driver's side of the boat.

You should also confirm that your boat's insurance covers you for towing skiers and inflatables.

Of course you can learn to ski before you set off behind your own boat, and there are many ski-lakes and schools up and down the country. Again the BWSF will provide you with a list of these. Tel: 01932 579931.

And finally for the real adrenaline junkies there is ski-racing. This is just what is says, with skiers being towed behind high-powered boats, racing against each other round circuits on lakes or the sea. Engine powers go right up to twin 250hp outboards, and speeds up to 100mph – only for the totally insane!

Cala Figuera, Mallorca. Photo by Tom Isitt

Chapter 10:
Towing

Having a trailable boat saves you money in storage and mooring fees and means you can explore distant waters or even take your boat abroad, but you must know the rules and regulations, and be able to handle your rig behind your car

One of the great advantages of owning a sportsboat or RIB is that most of them are light enough to be towed behind your own car or 4WD. This has two benefits. Firstly you save money because you do not need a berth in a marina, and secondly you can take your boat wherever you want, in the UK and abroad. Towing a boat is not difficult, after all a million or so caravanners tow much larger rigs all the time, but it is vital that you learn how to do it properly, and comply with the many laws that cover it.

In this Chapter we will present a guide to the towing regulations in the UK, at the start of 2012, as they affect most leisure users, however we must stress that we cannot cover every detail and aspect, and it is the responsibility of any driver to satisfy themselves that they comply with the law before travelling on the road.

Also major alterations to the regulations governing the manufacture of trailers are set to come into force in October 2012 and will apply to all trailers built after that

ate. Whilst complying with these will be the maker's responsibility, it is important that you make sure you ve buying a trailer that is lly type-approved. New quirements will include de-marker lights and some f the rear lights permanently xed to the trailer and wired a, which will therefore have to e waterproof. Existing trailers ill not be affected.

The full set of rules is covered a the Construction & Use egulations, 1986, and the Road ehicle Lighting Regulations, 989, both huge books. A more onvenient source of detailed information is the National railer and Towing Association, hose Guide to Safe & Legal owing is one of the most omprehensive you will find. ww.ntta.co.uk.

icence

he first requirement is the orrect driving licence. Anyone ith a normal driving licence, lled Cat B, obtained after 1st January 1997, is allowed to tow a trailer whose maximum weight, including boat and equipment does not exceed the unladen weight, or kerb weight of the towing vehicle, and the total weight of tow vehicle and trailer does not exceed 3.5tonnes.

If you take an extra one-hour test, your licence moves up to Cat B+E, and you are allowed to tow a rig whose combined weight does not exceed 8.25tonnes. though with the obvious proviso that the weight of trailer and boat must not exceed the vehicle manufacturer's recommended maximum towing weight.

Anyone with licence obtained before 1st January 1997 can automatically tow up to Cat B+E.

No learner driver or anyone with a provisional licence can tow anything.

Weights

It is now worth looking a little more closely at some of the definitions.

MGW is the Maximum Gross Weight, also called the Maximum Allowable Mass, MAM. For the towing vehicle this is the maker's stated maximum weight, which includes the vehicle, occupants and luggage. It should be found on the vehicle plate under the bonnet, and in the Owner's Manual. For the trailer, the MGW is the maker's maximum weight, which includes the trailer itself, plus the boat and its gear. This should be on a plate near the towbar.

Maximum recommended towing weight is the vehicle maker's recommended figure. If you exceed this, and are stopped, you will be prosecuted and fined, and will also find your insurance will be invalidated.

Kerb weight is the maker's stated weight of the vehicle, including a full fuel tank, plus toolkit, and sometimes including the driver.

It should also be noted that strictly according to the law, the MGW of the trailer is the figure on the plate, not its overall weight at any time. Thus if you are towing a trailer whose stated MGW exceeds your allowance, even if it is empty, or the boat on it is lighter than the maximum permitted, you will still be breaking the law.

For most saloon cars, the maker's recommended maximum is rarely more than the kerb weight, often less. For a modern medium sized saloon this will be around 1200kg. For larger saloons it will be 1500-1800kg. 4WDs however will usually have a maximum towing weight greater than their kerb weight, reflecting their greater towing capacity and power. A Freelander for instance can tow 2000kg, whereas the figures for the Discovery and Land Rover are 3500kg.

Sizes

The maximum length of trailer you can tow, excluding the drawbar and hitch is 7m. However, this is the trailer only, and the boat can overhang the rear, by up to 3.05m. If the overhang is greater than 1m,

Two-wheel trailers are ideal for boats up to 16-19ft. They are lighter than a four-wheel trailer, and easier to manoeuvre when they have been unhitched from the vehicle. They can be unbraked if their maximum gross weight is less than 50% of the weight of the tow vehicle, up to a maximum weight of trailer and boat of 750kg. In practice this means they should be used for boats up to around 400kg, or 12-14ft.

you must fix a red board or cloth to the back of the boat. If it is 2 - 3.05m you must have a correctly-sized and lit board. The overall length of car, trailer and boat must not exceed 18m.

The normal maximum width of the trailer is 2.55m, but the boat may overhand this by up to 305mm each side, to a maximum 2.9m. Above 2.9m, up to 4.3m you must carry special marker boards and lights, and inform the police.

There is no official maximum height, but the rig must be safe and stable at all times, and the normal recommended height is 3m, or 1.7 x the width across the wheels.

Lights

Every trailer must show lights to the rear at all times. These must include 2 red rear lights, 2 red brake lights, 2 orange indicator lights, 2 red warning triangles, 1 white number plate light, and at least one or two fog lights if the trailer is over 1.3m wide. The lights must be a maximum of 1.5m above the ground, though if the construction of the boat makes this impossible, this can be increased to 2.1m. A warning light or buzzer must be fitted inside the car, or on the dashboard, that works in unison with the indicators, and shows if either one of them has failed

If the trailer is over 5m long excluding the hitch, it must have at least one orange reflector each side, depending on the actual length. All trailers built after 1990 must have white reflectors showing to the front, and if they are more than 400mm wider than the front lights of the tow vehicle, either

side, they must show white lights forward.

Number Plate

The trailer must have a number plate that is the same size, shape, colour, and style as that on the rear of the car. Hand drawn versions are not allowed.

Brakes

You can tow an unbraked trailer up to 50% of the kerb weight of the tow vehicle, up to a maximum 750kg. Above this you must have overrun brakes, that activate when the car brakes. On trailers built after 1983 these must be hydraulically damped.

Breakaway cable

A braked trailer must have a breakaway cable connected to the car, which operates the hand-brake and stops the trailer if the tow hitch should jump off the ball. An unbraked trailer should have a similar chain or cable which keeps the two together under the same circumstances - and it can happen, either if the mechanism fails, or if you don't hook the hitch on properly.

Mirrors

You must have a clear view to the rear at all times, so if the trailer is wider than the car, you must fit extended wing mirrors while you are towing.

Mudguards

The trailer wheels must be shielded by mudguards. These can either be steel, or better still plastic which are less likely to cause damage if you should clip something while manoeuvring.

Tyres

Tyres can either be cross-ply or radial, but you must not mix the two on the same axle. They also don't have to be the same as on the car. They should be uprated to carry the load of the boat and trailer, usually meaning four-ply, six-ply or eight ply, as they can actually be carrying twice the load as those on your car. Because of this, van tyres are commonly used. The same regulations regarding tread depth and wear apply, plus you should look out for sidewall damage, as they are more likely to hit the kerb as you corner.

You are rarely likely to wear down the tread, but what does happen is that the rubber perishes with age, becoming dangerous. They can also perish if they are left standing in one position over winter, with the load on them. The answer is to jack them up at the end of the season, or even better, remove the wheels and help prevent the trailer being stolen.

A spare wheel is useful, but it must be securely locked in place, to prevent it being stolen and taken off when not in use.

Insurance

By law you must have third party cover for the trailer, as well as for the car. Make sure that your insurers know you will be towing. The boat insurance should cover the comprehensive aspect, but check all the same.

Parking

Some car-park bye-laws prohibit you from parking trailers in their bays, and parking meter regulations prevent you from straddling two bays with the car and trailer. If you need to park the trailer, it must be immobilised by either applying the handbrake, or chocking the wheels. At night, between the hours of sunset and sunrise, if it is on a public road it must be marked front and rear with lights, not just reflectors.

At home, you should check that local byelaws allow you to store the boat and trailer in your front garden. Your back garden is usually OK.

Right: Roller trailers make recovery easier, but they are more expensive than bunk trailers.

Nose-weight

This is the downward force that the trailer hitch applies to the towball. It is a vital safety aspect, keeping the boat stable when travelling on the road at speed. If you do not have sufficient nose-weight, the trailer can start to snake, or swerve from side to side, destabilising the whole rig. If this has ever happened to you, you will know how unnerving it can be. If you should feel it starting, do not brake, as this makes it worse. Instead lift your foot from the accelerator until your speed has reduced, and the snaking will stop.

Snaking occurs as you go faster, but it can be activated when another larger vehicle overtakes you. Increased nose-weight delays the onset. By law your trailer should have a minimum nose-weight of 4% of its all-up weight, or 25kg, which ever is greater. In practice, it is recommended the nose-weight be at least 50kg, preferably 75kg, though your car will have a maximum recommended figure. 100kg is usually deemed the maximum, as too great, and the steering will be affected, and the suspension could be damaged.

Nose-weight is governed by the position of the boat on the trailer fore-and-aft relative to the wheels, but is also affected by any gear inside it. You can check this with special balances, or just use your bathroom scales with a board across them. In practice if you can only just heft the weight of the hitch, then that is close to ideal. Get the boat correctly located, then fix the bow post at that position, but remember that two full fuel tanks right at the transom will change the figure completely. Try to store heavy items over the wheels.

Straps

Your boat should be securely held down at all times when you are underway. Ratchet straps are the only way to do this properly - don't use rope, as it will slacken as you drive and the boat bounces. For all except the smallest dinghies you should use two straps, front and rear, each with a minimum 1 tonne

breaking strain, and 50mm wide webbing. In addition you should hook on the winch strap, and tighten it, and finally take several turns of rope through the bow-eye down to the winch post for good measure.

When you are travelling at 60mph on the motorway, with cars all around you, and suddenly have to take avoiding action, you want to be completely confident that everything is securely attached behind you.

For preference take the straps over the gunwale and thread

them through the cleats, to prevent them slipping back or forwards. Make sure they are secured to the trailer, preferably through welded eyes, and cannot chafe as you drive. Secure the ends, if necessary wrapping them with several turns of duck tape, as the slipstream at speed will quickly have them flapping in the breeze behind you. A piece of old carpet will prevent any damage to the boat or the gunwale. On a RIB, with its rubber tubes, take the strap through the ski-hooks on the transom.

When launching you should reverse the rig down the slipway with the winch strap still attached, till the boat is partly in the water. Then partly lower the engine till the cooling water intakes are submerged, start it and let it warm up. If the water is shallow, push the boat gently off the trailer before engaging reverse, or the prop might hit the bottom.

Tow Hitches

Unless your vehicle has already got a tow-hitch on it, you will have to get one fitted. Don't even think about doing this yourself – it is too critical to the safety of your own car and other road users. But also the electrics and electronics on a modern car are so complex, that only an expert knows how to connect into them.

You can have one fitted by the vehicle manufacturer, either when you buy it or afterwards, but this is usually an expensive route. Specialist fitting companies do nothing but this, and you can get the details of your local ones from Yellow Pages or the Internet, or ask your trailer supplier who they recommend. Caravan dealers will also suggest local firms.

Right: A four-wheel trailer is better for boats over 19ft or so, especially those with heavier stern-drives. It has a greater carrying capacity, and gives greater safety in the event of a problem with one wheel or tyre. But it is heavier than a two-wheel trailer, and harder to move around when it is unhitched from the vehicle

Bottom Right: Always read the slipway instructions before using it

Driving tips

If you have never towed a boat before, there are some basic principles to remember. Your all-up weight will have nearly doubled, so the car will accelerate much slower, and take longer to brake, so you need to allow more time for all manoeuvres, especially pulling out and overtaking.

The overall length will be more than twice as much, and your width will probably have increased, so you need to allow for this when going through gaps. Pulling out round parked cars is especially tricky, as you need to swing out farther in advance to make sure the trailer clears. Similarly when going round corners, you need to swing out, though not so far that you impede oncoming vehicles.

Reversing is an art all of its own, and should be practised beforehand off the road on a quiet open space such as an empty car park, or field. On the road or in the marina it is safest if you have someone guiding you behind the trailer, to make sure everything is clear, and to watch all the corners.

Avoid busy town centres in the rush hour, or at night, as it is difficult to judge where other vehicles are around you. If you are in any doubt about a situation, stop and take stock rather than blundering in.

Speed limits

The maximum speed for any trailer on single carriageway roads in the UK with no lower speed limit is 50mph. On dual carriageways and motorways it is 60mph. Foreign limits vary, and you should check these before going abroad.

Maintenance

Even though it covers a comparatively low number of miles per year, correct maintenance of your trailer is essential, both for safety and convenience. In fact it is this low use that causes most or the problems, with items corroding and seizing up through lack of use, rather than wearing out. We cover the main points in Chapter 14, but here we should add the importance of flushing out the brakes and bearings if the trailer has been immersed in salt water, and letting them cool down after a run before launching. It is also important not to leave the hand-brake on for long periods, especially if the brakes are wet from launching, or over winter, as they can seize on. Chock the wheels instead.

Trailer types

A brief mention of the trailer types you will encounter is useful here. Unbraked trailers are simplest, cheapest and lightest, for boats up to around 400kg all up weight, providing the total weight of trailer and boat is not greater than 50% of your tow vehicle's kerb weight, with a maximum total weight of 750kg.

Above this you will need a braked trailer. For boats up to 1 tonne, a two-wheel trailer is suitable, and is easier to manoeuvre by hand. Above this you will need a four-wheel trailer, though remember this will be heavy in its own right, up to 500kg, which makes a significant impact on the all-up weight of the rig. It will also be harder to move around when not coupled to the car.

The roller type of trailer makes recovery easier than bunk types, but is heavier, and more expensive.

The trailer manufacturers will give you more advice on the best model for your particular requirements, but always remember to allow for extra gear and fuel when specifying your boat's weight.

Preflight check list:

Before you start driving, run through a simple checklist:

- ■ Secure the straps and the winch strap
- ■ Hook on the breakaway cable
- ■ Check all the lights work correctly
- ■ Tape the lighting board in place - these will always bounce off if you don't
- ■ Wind up the jockey wheel, and secured the handle to stop it winding down as you go
- ■ Secure any loose kit inside the boat Remove cushions and fasten the cover
- ■ Adjust your mirrors

Then five miles down the road, or at any convenient point, stop, get out and check nothing has moved. If it is going to come loose, it will be in the first few miles.

CHAPTER 11:
Where to go

Now you are ready to go, Tom Isitt talks you through the types of cruising areas in the UK, and gives you some of his favourite destinations

Okay, so you've bought your boat, you've kitted it and yourself out in all the necessary gear, you've done the training courses, and now you're ready to go. But, go where? To the nearest waterski lake? To the coast? Along the nearest river? Where is the best place to take your boat, and what should you do when you get there?

The real joy of sports boating is the freedom it gives you to explore. Just hitch up your trailer to the car, and off you go. Owners of bigger craft are pretty much stuck where they are, unless they want to undertake a lengthy (and expensive) sea voyage, but trailer-boaters can go where they like. Fancy a week boating in Cornwall? No problem…just hitch up and head for the South-West. Maybe a fortnight in the Western Isles of Scotland?

Jump in the car and away you go. And there are literally thousands of slipways available for you to use (check out The Good Launch Guide, price £9.95 for the most comprehensive guide to launch sites around the UK. Or go to www.boatlaunch.co.uk).

The world, in theory, is your oyster. But before planning a trailer-boating holiday to the Aral Sea or the outer islands of the Hebrides, a bit of experience gained closer to home might be a good idea. So, a few decisions need to be made about the sort of boating you want to do.

For a start, is your boat suitable for the trips you want to undertake? A flat-bottomed bass-boat isn't going to be ideal for crossing the Channel in a Force 4. And a deep-vee monohull with a five-litre petrol engine might not be the ideal choice for river cruising.

You also need to think about your crew…are they

any use at all, or are they just friends along for a pleasant day out, who don't know the difference between a bowline and a bight? Every boat that is going to sea needs at least one other crew member (apart from you, the skipper) who can assist with mooring, navigation, and even take the helm if you knock yourself unconscious or fall overboard. As we have told you in the Training Chapter, it is a good idea to get all the members of your family to do an RYA Level 2 Powerboat course so that there is another person on board who knows what you are doing, and can give you a break from the helm, or take over in an emergency.

Rivers

The reason you bought a sportsboat in the first place, presumably, is to zoom around at speed, possibly with a view to doing a bit of waterskiing, or towing the kids behind the boat in a ringo. If this is the case, then non-tidal rivers, or canals, aren't really going to suit you or your boat for much of the time. They will have speed limits, of 4-8mph, which do not really suit large engines and deep vee hulls. But they can make a pleasant change from going to sea, especially in a spell of bad weather and when visiting parts of the coast it is always nice to explore any rivers you come across.

But larger rivers, in their tidal sections can make good cruising grounds round Britain.

For instance there is no speed limit on the Thames downstream of Wandsworth Bridge, and in theory you

Pubs are favourite destinations, and the Cresselly Arms at Cresswell Quay in Milford Haven is one of the delights of this hidden gem of a waterway. But don't get caught by the tide as it drops, and remember that alcohol and safe boating do not mix

...an zip under Tower Bridge
t 20 knots (just don't cause
xcessive wash, and be careful
o navigate properly and safely.
Also be very careful of the
waves thrown up by the large
passenger trip boats on the
ver, especially where they
ounce back from the walls in
he narrow sections).

And actually, the tidal part
f the Thames is a fascinating
place to go boating, with 2000
years of history right there
(although don't go too close
to the Houses of Parliament
or you'll find yourself the
centre of unwanted attention
from military types in black
RIBs bristling with guns). St
Paul's, The Globe Theatre,
Tower Bridge, The Dome, the
pubs of Wapping (including
the gibbet outside the Prospect
of Whitby), Big Ben, the
London Eye, Canary Wharf,
and most spectacularly of all,
the Thames Barrier...all these
have a completely different
perspective from a small boat
on the river. Finding anywhere
to moor up is tricky, but it's
worth a taking a trip down
Britain's oldest navigable
waterway. There are slipways
of varying quality all along
the tidal Thames where you
can launch, but it's advisable
to plan carefully — on Spring
tides the river can flow pretty
quickly.

Our favourite is Putney
Hard, which has plenty of
room, and space to leave
your car and trailer at the top,
though beware Spring Tides,
or you can return to find the
water lapping up your doors.
From here, once you have
passed under Wandsworth
Bridge, where the 8mph limit
stops, it is a superb 45 minute
dash down to the Thames
Barrier. You have also got Chas
Newens' excellent sportsboat
emporium adjacent with
spares and advice. The Port of
London Authority controls the
tidal river, and has leaflets and
information. **www.pla.co.uk**

Above Teddington the river
is non-tidal, with 45 locks along
its 125 mile length, and a 5mph
speed limit, but the reward
is beautiful scenery, and
the chance to visit Windsor,
Runnymede, Henley and
Oxford by water. You will need
a licence, but there are plenty

Above: The Western
isles of Scotland
are delightful and
unspoilt, but you
do need to be
experienced to take
your boat there

Left: Lymington is a
popular destination,
and one of the many
safe harbours that
make the Solent one
of our most popular
cruising areas for
novices and experts
alike. Though expect
to find it busy in the
height of Summer

Above: Bosham is a delightful waterside village in Chichester Harbour, but it does dry out, and the Harbour has an overall speed limit

Right: Travelling through the heart of our Capital in your own boat gives a whole new perspective on the many familiar landmarks, and at present there is no speed limit, so provided you navigate safely, you can plane past the Houses of Parliament, right down to the Thames Barrier. But beware the tide can run fast, particularly through the bridges, and there are few places to stop or moor

of slipways, and waterside pubs. The Environment Agency control the non-tidal river

There is a certain amount of boating that goes on in other British rivers, such as the Severn, the Trent, the Humber and the Yorkshire Ouse, while the Scottish Lochs, and especially the Caledonian Canal have wide open waters.

Lakes

For many people, lakes are a great way of getting into boating. They don't have tides, or very big waves, there are few navigational hazards, and it's quite hard to get lost. So for many beginners, the reassurance afforded by lake boating, with the shore always within sight make lakes a great starting point.

The down side in the UK is that fewer and fewer lakes will allow you to travel at planing speeds. In the good old days you could stick your boat on pretty much any stretch of inland water and zip about, but now there are relatively few places you can do that. The Lake District, traditional stomping ground for fast boats, is now effectively out of bounds for powerboaters. Ullswater, Coniston and now Windermere all have 10mph speed limits but even so, the magical scenery still makes them worth visiting.

This leaves just the Scottish lochs as the only large stretche of UK inland water you can go boating at speed on. Loch Lomond and Loch Ness are still currently available (although this may not remain the case for much longer). Loch Lomond, particularly, is a popular destination for sportsboaters, with good facilities at the northern end.

Finally, there are privately-owned lakes with waterski and boating clubs, where, for an

annual membership, you can take your sportsboat. You can find these all over the country, with large clubs at Tallington and Tattershall in Lincolnshire, Church Wilne in the Midlands, and a number of them around the peripheries of the M25. Most of these places will allow members to launch and use their boats on the lake, and some also have static caravans or lodges where members can stay for the weekend (or longer), creating little boating and watersports communities. These are a great way of getting some on-water time, meeting other like-minded souls, and gaining an insight into the social side of boating. The British Waterski Federation will give you a list.

Ultimately, lake boating is a good introduction to life on the water, allowing you to practise your techniques of launching and driving your boat in controlled conditions, but for many people it is too restrictive. There are fairly limited horizons, even on a large stretch of water like Loch Lomond, so unless your aspirations go no further than waterskiing or towing a ringo, you will want to look farther afield.

Coastal

For most people, the limitless possibilities of boating on the sea are what really appeal. You can either moor your boat permanently afloat in a marina, or take a summer berth, or trail it either to the same slipway, or a different location every trip. Being an island, we have thousands of miles of coastline where we can launch our boats and go exploring. Anyone watching the Coast series on television cannot fail to be fascinated by the places you can reach.

Of course coastal boating requires a significantly greater level of expertise than any kind of inland boating, and the risks are higher, but potentially the rewards are greater, too - seeing your first dolphin breaking the surface just off your port bow, and swimming along with you, making your first Channel crossing, catching a string of mackerel, or just watching the

sun setting over a peaceful anchorage. These are the moments that give boating on the sea its appeal.

The downside (if you can call it that) is that there's a lot more to sea boating. You need to be a lot more clued up on tides, chart-work, weather, navigation, mechanics and boat-handling. But if, at first glance, this all seems a bit of a chore, be assured that it becomes immensely rewarding as you start to get to grips with it all. And as you become more comfortable with it, after a couple of seasons you can be navigating around our coasts with the assurance of a pro.

For the relative novice, it's probably a good idea to start somewhere where you don't get a 40ft tidal range or a 5-knot tide running. You might want to avoid the Scilly Isles or the Channel Islands until you have a few more sea-miles under your belt. Poole Harbour is a popular place to get a taste of salt water…it's well protected, blessed with great boating facilities (including numerous slipways) and relatively free of hazards. The Solent is another good starting point. The shore is always in sight, though beware the tides, which can flow fast, and catch you out when you return to the launch site. There is an abundance of marinas and boating facilities, and there are plenty of other boats around to help or to practice your collision regs with.

What is important, though, is to have a thorough knowledge of the area you're boating in. A nautical almanac with tide tables and detailed port information is essential, as a comprehensive set of up-to-date charts. On top of that, a GPS (or two) with spare batteries is pretty useful, plus essential spares for your boat. If you're not the most technically-minded of individuals, you might consider joining SeaStart, www.seastart.co.uk. They are a marine breakdown service who will come out in a boat and either fix your vessel if it breaks down, or tow you back to port if they can't fix it out on the water. If you're going any

distance, a written passage-plan is essential, with notes of tide times and heights, harbour info, emergency numbers and contact details.

And finally

Ultimately, it doesn't matter where you take your boat, as long as you take it somewhere. Too many people end up with their boat parked on a trailer in the drive, never actually using it. And that would be a chronic waste, because there's a whole world out there waiting to be explored. Whether it's a stretch of local river or a cross-Channel jaunt, getting out in your boat and enjoying it is what sportsboating is all about. Some people are happy to launch and go boating in the same area, year after year, others prefer to use their boats to explore this fantastic island where we live. Either way, there is nothing quite so satisfying as arriving somewhere unfamiliar by water, knowing you've done a good job with your navigation and seamanship.

You might also think about joining a sportsboat club such as Pathfinder Powerboat Club, www.ppc.org.uk. These clubs run regular events where you can get together with other boaters. Here you will meet people who are only too pleased to pass on their experience and expertise to newcomers, and even total novices will find themselves being welcomed into the fold.

And lastly, don't forget to check out Powerboat & RIB Magazine for the latest news for sportsboaters and regular articles on sportsboat-friendly destinations, both inland and coastal.

A 4WD makes launching on steep and slippery slipways easier, but you should still check carefully that they have enough depth of water, and do not drop off at their ends

Here are just a few possible launch sites to get you started

Poole Harbour
Salterns Marina

■ Concrete slip, onto mud, available two hours either side of high water. Not ideal for larger (over 24ft) craft, but there are hoist facilities for larger craft. Day launch and recovery costs £32, and there is ample parking for car and trailer. Marine has excellent facilities including changing room and showers. The on-site hotel has a good bar and restaurant, and makes a pleasant place to stay overnight.

Salterns Marina: 01202 709971

Hamble, Southampton
Warsash Public Hard

■ A firm gravel public slip available (free) at all states of tide, although it's a bit soft at low-water Springs, with enough room for several boats to launch simultaneously. Free parking 100 yards along lane, as well as toilets. The Rising Sun pub opposite is the ideal place for a sundowner at the end of the day. Can get quite busy at peak times in the summer.

Milford Haven
Milford Haven Port

■ Another of Britain's great natural harbours, Milford Haven in South Wales is a true hidden gem. Up to three miles wide, and 25 miles long to the head of navigation, the lower reaches are home to huge oil terminals, and massive tankers and car ferries come in day and night. For this reason the lower stretches have no speed limits, making this a sportsboaters paradise, though you must pay great attention to the huge sea-going vessels, which have right of way at all times. It may be 200 miles from London, but it is nearly all motorway, making it easy to reach. There are several excellent slipways and marinas.

Milford Haven Port Authority:
01646 696100. www.mhpa.co.uk

Mersea Island, Essex
West Mersea

■ The East Coast rivers and estuaries have a fascination all of their own, and are largely unspoilt. The tidal ranges and shallow beaches mean that access is not easy, and large areas dry out, but you can launch a small RIB or sportsboat and have lots of fun exploring, if you check your charts carefully. Mersea Island is cut off at the highest Spring tides, but is a popular spot, and gets very busy at weekends with tourists from all over the world visiting the oyster and lobster restaurants.

West Mersea Town Council
01206 382128
www.westmersea.org.uk

Pwllheli, North Wales
Public Slip

■ Excellent public concrete slip available at all states of tide giving access to sheltered water. The ramp is concrete onto mud and launching costs £8 a day, payable at the harbour master's office next to it. There are toilets and showers, and plenty of free parking.

Harbour Office: 01758 704081

Salcombe, Devon
Salcombe Harbour

■ This superb natural harbour has several launch sites, and many beautiful beaches and places to visit, though there is a speed-limit throughout the harbour. Salcombe itself has an excellent slipway, with pontoons alongside, but it does get busy in the summer. Kingsbridge, at the head of the harbour has another excellent slipway and car park alongside, but access is only 2-3 hours either side of high water. Or you can follow the creeks on a rising tide up to South Pool and Frogmore, but don't tarry too long in the pubs, or you will return to find your boat dried out.

Harbour Office: 01548 843791
harbour@southhams.gov.uk
www.salcombeinformation.co.uk

Calshot
Calshot Activities Centre

■ Located in the old sea-plane base, at the west end of Southampton Water, this has a superb concrete slip, accessible at all but the lowest spring tides. It gives you access to the whole of the Solent, and has good parking for car and trailer, excellent shoreside facilities, and some year-round boat parking. Charges are £14/day for a 6m boat, £330/yr up to 5.5m, £420/yr up to 6.5m.

Calshot Activities Centre: 02380 892077.
www.calshot.com

Weymouth
Weymouth Town Slipway

■ An excellent modern concrete slipway, launching into the sheltered harbour, and giving access to Lyme Bay, or the nearby Portland Harbour. Small boats up to 5m can use it at all states of the tide, larger boats most of the tide. Charge is £9/day for launch and recovery, £4.50 for the trailer, with a public car park nearby.

www.weymouth.gov.uk
01305 838000

Nothing beats tying up in front of a Mediterranean restaurant in your own boat – but practise your stern-to mooring if you want to really impress the other diners!

CHAPTER 12:
Going abroad

So you have mastered your boat-handling, and had a season in the UK, but now you want to broaden your horizons, Tom Isitt tells you what you need to know, and describes some of his favourite destinations

Despite being surrounded by some of the most beautiful coastline in the world, we Brits occasionally feel the need for some guaranteed sunshine and a decent meal. So we head for the Continent, where boating can be fantastic. The novelty of being in a completely different country is reason enough, but when you combine that with excitement of exploring a foreign coastline, provisioning at unfamiliar shops, and dropping anchor in a deserted sun-drenched cove with a sandy beach lapped by azure seas then you have a recipe for a great time.

Adventurous (and experienced) souls may chose to cross the Channel on their own bottoms - to use the correct nautical term, heading for the Normandy coast and the delights of Honfleur or St Malo, but you should only attempt this if you have a decent amount of sea-miles under your belt, and are in a well-found craft, typically 24ft upwards. Ideally, you would want to do the crossing in company with another boat, and you' should have a twin-engine craft (or at least one with an auxiliary outboard). The Channel is one of the busiest shipping lanes in the world, and you don't want to be out there broken down.

For the relative novice, the more sensible option is to trail your boat abroad. You can get across the Channel by ferry for under £200 return for two adults, two kids and a trailer, although the same will cost double on the Eurotunnel. From Calais you can head for the inland waters of Holland or south to the sun. If you want a shortcut to Spain, a ferry to Bilbao or Santander will cost around £650 and will save you a long drive.

Once you're abroad, the trick is not to hurry, and to be flexible. Everything will take longer than you expect, and if you try to cram too much in, you are likely to come unstuck. Be realistic with your itinerary because in some places it can take several hours just to find the man with the keys to the slipway barrier, or the petrol pump attendant who also runs the local charcuterie. You

eed to be adaptable, and not
et stressed if things don't go
ompletely according to plan.
We have trailed boats to
Iorth and Western France,
tlantic Spain and the Costas,
nd the Cote d'Azur of France,
nd not once did anything
o exactly to plan. But you
hink on your feet, adapt, and
etermine to enjoy it no matter
hat. And when you finally
everse your boat down a
ipway on the French Riviera
nd head off for lunch in
annes or St Tropez, then you
ealise that it really is worth the
ffort.

Rules and regulations

ut if there is a drawback
o boating abroad, it's the
aperwork. In the UK we take
 for granted that we don't
eed much documentation to
o boating. It's one of the few
astimes unfettered by rules
nd regulations foisted on us
y our Nanny State. But on
he Continent you'll find that
oating is a far more controlled
astime, and you'll need reams
f paperwork with you if you
re not to fall foul of the local
fficials.
There is not room in a
elatively all-encompassing

book such as this to list the
precise requirements of each
European country when it
comes to boating, so we suggest
you join the Royal Yachting
Association (it costs around £30
a year) and then avail yourself
of their expertise. Their web
site has (in the members-only
section) all the info you could
ever need about boating in
Europe. You can even find
country-specific regulations
covering trailing abroad.
And you will need to know
them, because it appears that
every country is different...
did you know that Italy has
a 12m maximum permissible
car/trailer length, whereas
in Holland it's 18m? Or that
in Germany a fully-laden
unbraked trailer must weigh
no more than 50 percent of the
weight of the towing vehicle,
plus 37.5kg?

Paperwork

It's time to get over your
very British distrust of
paperwork. Most foreigners
find it extraordinary that we
don't have to carry ID cards
or driving licences, because
in continental Europe you are
generally required to keep all
that sort of thing on you at all

times. And if you take your
boat abroad and don't have the
correct documents you risk the
possibilities of your boat being
impounded and significant
fines.
When using a UK-flagged
boat abroad you will need
papers both for the boat and
for the crew on board. There
is a core set of paperwork –
grandiosely called your ship's
papers – which, together with
your passport, should keep
you and your boat out of the
clutches of over-zealous foreign
officials.

Ship's Papers
Your Ship's Papers must all
be original documents (NOT
photocopies) and comprise:

Registration Document
Registration of non-commercial
pleasure craft is not compulsory
for a UK Citizen who keeps
their boat in the UK, but it is
compulsory if you want to take
your boat abroad. And herein
lies your first problem —boats
in the UK don't come with a
registration document like a
car, but you need one abroad.
The simple answer is to register
your boat on the Small Ships
Register (SSR), something
which can be done online at
https://mcanet.mcga.gov.uk/
ssr/ssr/ and which costs the
princely sum of £25. For this
you get an SSR number which
you stick on your transom,
and a registration document.
When abroad, you must
be prepared to present the
original registration document -
photocopies are not acceptable.

Ship Radio Licence
Under the International Radio
Regulations, a UK registered
vessel must have a Ship Radio
Licence if it is to install or use
radio equipment (including
a VHF or DSC radio, Radar,
EPIRB, etc). The licence, which
details the equipment covered,
must be carried onboard.

Insurance
Although technically you don't
have to have insurance for your
boat in the UK, it is nonetheless
advisable, and in Europe it is
virtually compulsory, and many
officials will ask for evidence of
insurance cover. Some countries

Above: Croatia is a
long haul by road,
but worth it for the
delightful waterside
villages and moorings

specify minimum levels of
cover, and some require a
translation, which your insurer
should be able to provide. You
should check the territorial
limits of your cover before
undertaking any trip, as you
may need to extend the cruising
limits.

Proof of VAT Status
EU residents may only use a
boat within the EU if it is VAT
paid or deemed to be VAT paid.
Therefore, although proof of
the VAT status of the vessel
is not actually part of a ship's
papers, it is needed to prove
that the boat is entitled to free
movement throughout the EU.
A customs officer is entitled to
ask you to prove the VAT status
of your boat and your boat
could be detained if its VAT
status is in doubt. If your vessel
was built or imported into the
EEA after 16th June 1998, you
will also need proof that your
vessel is RCD Compliant. The
original purchase invoice will
show that VAT has been paid.

Personal papers
Passport
Every crew member on board
requires a passport. If you
are cruising outside the EU
you may also need a visa. It is
advisable to check well before
you intend to leave the UK
as these can take time to get.
Within the EU if you have a
non-EU citizen onboard the
vessel, you will need to declare

them, even if the vessel itself
is entitled to free transit. You
should also check if they
require a visa.

Certificate of Competence
In UK waters the skipper of a
UK registered non-commercial
pleasure craft under 24m in
length is not required to have
a certificate of competence or
licence, unless the vessel is over
80 Gross Tonnes However this
is not necessarily the case in
the territorial waters of another
country. The requirements
vary from country to country
so you should establish
what is required in advance.
It is advisable to carry any
certificates you hold (just in
case) even if they are not a
requirement. The International
Certificate of Competence (ICC)
is increasingly the certificate
that is requested, but it is not a
boating licence. You can get an
ICC from the RYA for £38 if you
have a Powerboat Level 2 or
higher qualification.

Maritime Radio Operator's
Certificate of Competence
The International Radio
Regulations state that a
maritime radio may only
be used by the holder of a
Maritime Radio Operator's
Certificate of Competence
or by someone who is under
the direct supervision of
such a holder. The minimum

certificate of competence
required is the Short Range
Certificate for VHF/DSC
(or the old Restricted VHF
Operator for the old style
VHF only sets). However it is
permitted to monitor the radio
for safety purposes, or to use
it to request assistance in an
emergency without a Certificate
of Competence and Authority
to Operate.

Country-Specific
Documentation and
Publications
A country may specify
requirements such as a crew
list or specific publications
that must be carried (eg a
local almanac or a copy of the
Col-Regs). It is a good idea to
compile a crew-list anyway,
detailing the personal details
(date of birth, passport number
etc), and print off half a dozen
copies that can be handed over
to customs officials (this can
save laborious copying-out).
Vessels navigating European
inland waters are generally
required to carry a copy of
the local rules (which may be
written in the native language
of the country concerned). It
is important to ensure you are
aware of all such requirements
and details are available to RYA
members.

Flags
It is essential that you fly your
national ensign, and for all
British vessels this is the red
ensign (not the Union Flag). It
is also polite, but not obligatory
when visiting the waters of
another country, to fly the
maritime ensign of that country
as a mark of courtesy. This is
a sign that you acknowledge
that you are in their waters and
claim protection from the law of
the seas. In some areas you will
score brownie points for flying
the local flag, such as a Catalan
flag in places like Barcelona,
or the Corsican Turk's head
flag when in Corsica, but be
very careful that you have got
it right, and if in doubt, don't.
This isn't obligatory, but the
locals will look favourably
on you if you demonstrate an
understanding of their local
politics and culture.

Red diesel

This probably doesn't apply to many sportsboats, but if you have a diesel engine in your boat and use red diesel in the UK you should keep receipts for your fuel purchases in the UK and log them together with your engine hours, in order to demonstrate, should you be asked, that your red diesel purchases were legitimate. Boaters visiting Holland and Germany have been heavily fined recently for being unable to prove their red diesel was bought legally in the UK.

WHERE TO GO?

So, you've joined the RYA and mastered the rules and regs of the countries you intend visiting, you've told your insurance company what you're going to do, and you've assembled the paperwork necessary to keep yourself and your boat out of the clutches of foreign officials. All that's left now is to pick a destination and start planning.

We have a couple of favourites that will get you started, or UK boating magazines regularly feature reader's trips.

Honfleur
Normandy, France
49° 25' 47N 0° 13' 51E

If Disney were to create their own French sea-side town theme-park, you can bet it would be very similar to Honfleur, because this Normandy port is picture-postcard quaint. Sitting on your boat in La Vieux Bassin (the inner harbour) you couldn't be anywhere other than in northern France. The tall colourful buildings, the cafes and restaurants, the art galleries…it's all so Gallic, the only thing missing is the man on a bicycle with a string of onions.

From Honfleur you can meander your way along the Normandy coast, taking a look at the remains of the Mulberry Harbour and the D-Day beaches, an experience that is quite different from a boat to how it feels from land. It's all do-able in day-trips, or you could stop over at St Vaast and come back the next day. Or you could just loaf around in Honfleur eating and drinking in fine style.

Santa Margherita Ligure
North-west coast of Italy
44° 19' 50N 9° 12' 55E

The Italian Riviera is sophisticated, picturesque, and a boater's paradise. Not as snooty as the French Riviera, and with considerably nicer scenery, the stretch of coast either side of Genoa is gorgeous. Just to the south of Genoa, tucked into a charming bay, lie Rapallo and Santa Margherita Ligure, two jewels in the crown of the Italian Riviera.

Although a good two-day drive from the UK, the Italian Riviera is fabulous. Santa Margherita has a slightly faded elegance to it, but is blessed with excellent boating facilities and a very pleasant town (with some superb restaurants and bars). Nearby Rapallo is bigger and busier, and Portofino (just to the south) is a must-visit place by boat, if only to gawp at the superyachts before heading somewhere where a primo latte costs less than 10 euros.

Saint Raphael
Cote d'Azur, France
43° 24' 41N 6° 46' 53E

The Cote d'Azur is fabulous, but it does tend to be a bit snobbish. Monaco is so snooty there is actually a byelaw that prevents residents from shopping at Matalan, and Saint Tropez won't let you within the city limits unless you're wearing a Rolex. That's perhaps slightly exaggerated, but you wouldn't be surprised. But the Cote d'Azur is nonetheless definitely worth a visit.

The chances of getting in to Antibes or Nice are low, so head for Saint Raphael instead…it's a great town, the facilities are good, and it won't cost a fortune. Now get out in your boat and explore. St Tropez is definitely worth a visit, and if you're in a small boat they can usually squeeze you in for a couple of hours. Round the headland on Pamplonne Beach is where the beautiful people go to admire themselves and pay €200 a head for lunch in the beach restaurants. Heading east, Cannes, Antibes and Nice are all worth a visit, and places like St Jean Cap Ferrat and Villefranche-sur-Mer still look like a movie set, where you expect to see David Niven or Sophia Loren at any moment.

Barcelona
Spain
41° 22' 20N 2° 10' 56E

The thing about Barcelona is that the onshore fun is every bit as good (and probably better) than the onwater life. Putting it bluntly, the coast either side of Barcelona isn't the kind of cala-infested delight you will find elsewhere in Spain, but it is more than compensated for by being one of the coolest cities in Europe. Coast hopping will take you to some nearby stopping-places with some decent berthing opportunities, but you'll also have fun exploring the city of Barcelona — stroll the Ramblas, eat tapas, check out the bonkers Gaudi architecture, hit the shops and go to the Camp Nou (where Barcelona play football).

Puerto Cabopino, on Spain's Costa del Sol is a hidden gem in the midst of the package holiday beaches, with a marina and plenty of restaurants

CHAPTER 13:
Racing

Above: The Formula Honda Series, which ran for six years, provided exciting offshore racing, with identical hulls and engines, and the winning down to the skill of the crew. It has now become the P1 Superstock Series, using the same identical hulls, but with one class using 150hp Honda engines, and the larger boats using 300hp Mercury engines.

Have you thought of going powerboat racing, or even just watching it? John Cooke tells you how you can go about it

For many sportsboat owners, the ultimate thrill on the water is powerboat racing. You may just want to watch this exciting sport, or even take part in it yourself. You may even be able to take part in some races in your own sportsboat or RIB. Whichever, we show you where you can see it or even join in.

National offshore powerboat racing

Like yacht racing, powerboat racing is governed in the UK by the Royal Yachting Association www.rya.org.uk at national level, and the UIM (Union International Motonautique) at International level. Between them they make the rules that govern the sport, to keep it safe for spectators and competitors alike, as well as fair for everyone.

The inshore and circuit-racing classes usually only have a driver, whilst the offshore classes have a driver and a navigator. When you get up to the largest offshore boats like P1 and Class 1 you have a set-up where the driver steers and the throttle man is responsible for the engine throttles and trimming the boat with trim tabs and ballast.

The RYA publish an event calendar on their website.

Getting started

There are several routes to getting into powerboat racing, and in many of the classes, boats can be used for recreational purposes as well as racing. Some of the National races have separate 'Basic races' which can be entered with a ski boat or RIB and some specified items

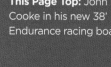

and P1 Superstock have races as far North as Scotland and even the Isle of Man – see the RYA website for details. www.rya.org.uk

Races

As we have said, many of the calendar events also hold Basic Races, which anyone can enter with pretty much any boat that will fit loosely into an existing class. Classes are usually defined by engine power or capacity. For more information, call or email the RYA and direct your enquiry to the powerboat racing department, or get in touch with the club organising the event – they are always willing to help newcomers.

Offshore Circuit Racing

This class is based on ski boats, and is by far the easiest to get into as a weekend racer. The class was dominated for many years by Phantom ski boats, but now there are Bernicos and Concordes racing in two classes, 1.3litre and 1.8litre. Yamaha engines dominate both classes, with the 140hp and 90hp engines being used. With speeds of up to 60mph and a starting price of £3,000 for a secondhand rig, this is a very cheap way to go racing. As with everything now green engines are coming into the sport and you can run a more powerful "EPA" motor such as the Evinrude 150HO.

Just as Kart racing has

safety equipment such as ...ddles, flares, bilge pump, a ...ving line, and some personal ...uipment such as whistle, knife, ...ecial race lifejackets and crash ...lmets. Sometimes clubs can ...d equipment that you can ...rrow from other competitors – ...y really are a friendly crowd! ...e cost of a licence (which ...ludes third party insurance) ...75 per person (driver and ...vigator) for one race, plus the ...ry fee for the event of £75

to £100 for the boat. An annual licence for the season is £320

One of the great attractions of powerboat racing is that it is usually free for the public to come along and watch, and many of the venues provide all sorts of entertainment to keep the public amused when there isn't something going on on the water.

Venues

Much of the Offshore racing in the UK is based on the South Coast, with events stretching from Cornwall to Kent, but some classes such as Thundercats, OCR

Left: OCR classes are the cheapest and easiest way to go racing, with basic ski-boats, and standard outboards, either 70hp or 140hp

Bottom: The third Round Britain Powerboat race in 2008 brought together boats and crews from around the world, with speeds up to 100mph, and gruelling stages over a ten-day period. The eventual winner, Blue FPT, designed by Italian legend Fabio Buzzi averaged 75mph for the 1500 miles, and its crew included veteran British navigator Dag Pike, at 75 the oldest competitor in the race

Right: Another Round Britain Powerboat Race entrant in 2008 was this Scorpion Cabin RIB, crewed by Sarah Jane Fraser and Miranda Knowles

helped future Grand Prix stars learn their motor racing craft, so does OCR lead drivers to higher classes, with a short, tight circuits, which allow spectators to view the whole course, and with heats over two days racing that means there is lots to see. From a competitor's point of view, the boats can be used for water skiing and general family fun, so it is not just used for racing.
Go to www.ocrda.org for more

Class III

This is the main 'proper' race boat class, and competitors race at National, European and World levels. The Batboat design has dominated at all levels of the sport for quite a few years with catamarans sharing the spoils. The old Mercury 2litre XR2 engines used to dominate, but they have all but disappeared now, to be replaced by the more eco-friendly 2.5litre XS200. With these engines the boats are capable of speeds into the high seventies, and the catamarans in perfect conditions are hitting over 90mph. Just like OCR these boats race around a circuit, but with more complicated courses and further offshore. They are mostly tandem seating boats and can only carry two people, so not the best for water skiing on a Sunday afternoon, but they are fast! www.orda.co.uk

V24

The V24 offshore powerboat was designed by Ocke Mannerfelt and is protected by a Design Patent. It is a one-design race boat, with a hull that is just under 8 metres long and powered by a 5.7litre petrol V8 sterndrive giving 320hp. Although this is a Volvo Penta supplied engine and drive, it's heritage is an American Chevrolet V8 and it sounds like it! When a few of these boats are racing together you will usually hear them before you see them. In one-design racing, no alterations are allowed to be made to hull or engine, making the racing fair and close but more importantly everyone has the potential to win. The results depend on the skill and determination of the driver and co-driver and not on their budget. www.v24club.com

Main Picture: Zapcats are cheap, fast and thrilling

Powerboat P1 SuperStock

When the giant outboard manufacturer Honda expanded their range of engines into higher powers, they decided to support a racing series that would showcase their units, and at the same time draw in new drivers, sponsors and spectators to the sport. They ended up with two one-design classes, 150hp and 225hp, using standard Cougar-designed hulls and standard engines. The classes provided thrilling close-quarter racing, and introduced a whole new group of drivers, crews and spectators to offshore racing. After six successful years Honda withdrew their support in 2009, but the classes were re-organised under the title Powerboat P1 SuperStock Series. P1 have now introduced their own 28' hull into the series and coupled with Evinrude 250 HO power this is now the new premier class, coupled with jet sport racing their events are definitely a spectacle.

The 21ft 150hp was the starter class. With speeds of over 50mph, they weren't super fast, but as a one-design class, the racing was always close. New boats started at around £34,000 but secondhand rigs were available for considerably less, depending on their racing pedigree.

The larger and faster class had a twin-stepped hull, and now uses Mercury 300hp engines. With speeds in the 70s it is faster, but the racing is just as close as the smaller boats. With the races getting good television coverage, and

without committing the capital investment in a race boat. www.p1superstock.co.uk

RIB Racing

The RIB class has changed a number of times over the years, going from racing around the UK to racing with the Class III boats, and is now turning into more of a long-distance class once again. With the second ever Round Britain Race in 2008, RIBs came of age, proving themselves to be tough, seaworthy and fast, and finishing high amongst the entrants in this gruelling 1200-mile event. The British Inflatable Boat Owners Association has a full calendar of races, cruises and family trips. www.biboa.com

Thunderkids Class and UK Formula Future

This is where the kids can start from as young as 10 years old, with classes for different age groups from 10 years and over in the S250 class they race a

12ft single-seater Sorceror with a 25hp outboard. Then for 12 years and over in the F400 class there are the 14ft Fletchers with 40hp outboards, For 16 years and over the class is E900 with boats from 16ft to 17ft and the Evinrude 90hp ETEC engine, and lastly for aged 17 and over there is the E1500 Class which have hulls from 18ft to 20ft with the Evinrude 150hp HO engine. There is a natural progression from class to class with the classes overlapping, so that you can move up at your own pace. The club hold regular training sessions at the beginning of the season for newcomers, and are very welcoming to beginners. www.ukformulafutureoffshore raceclub.co.uk www.thundertour.co.uk

Thundercats

Inflatable catamaran racing began in South Africa in the early 1980s when local crews raced inflatable boats down treacherous rivers and along the rugged coastline. Since the days of those extreme thrill-

he series traveling round the oast of the UK, stopping at easide resorts on the way it vas probably one of the easiest lasses to get sponsorship or the boats. P1 even offer easing deals for people vanting to get into the sport

seeking pioneers, inflatable boat technology has come a long way and the sport has crossed the oceans of the world, they now race in South Africa, Australia and New Zealand.

Thundercat racing is an open class that allows any make of homologated 750cc, 50hp engine that fits within the rules and specifications to race, thus giving competitive and inexpensive racing for the drivers and an exciting spectator sport.

This type of racing came to the UK and Channel Isles as an existing class approximately six years ago, slowly but surely the series has taken foot and this year the first ever World Championships were staged in the UK and a British team came second.

The Thundercat racing series takes place on freshwater lakes, rivers and dams or on the sea. Courses are M-shaped, and bring the public within feet from the action.

This is competition not for the faint-hearted and the team must work together to be as one with the boat. Both the Pilot and Co-Pilot are paramount to maximise the speed and ability to win. On land the nearest sport to this would be motorcycle side-car racing. It gives you the power-to-weight-ratio better than a Ferrari 350 at the cost of a Robin Reliant! Once again this is one of those craft that you can also take out for a spin at the weekend with some friends, and not just use for competition.

Zapcats

Just like their cousins the Thundercats, the Zapcats are developed from life saving surf rescue craft for racing and leisure, Zapcats are designed to cope with a huge variety of sea conditions from flat calm lakes to large breaking surf.

Zapcats race in small packs, hitting speeds of around 50mph. The 50hp engine gives the boat a power-to-weight ratio of 340bhp per tonne putting in the same league as super-cars and the Zapcats can outmanoeuvre any boat of a similar size. The pilots and co-pilots are subjected to up to twice the force of gravity in the tightest of turns providing a thrilling, high-octane sport for the growing numbers of spectators following the sport.

The Zapcat National Championships attracts a wide variety of competitors from all manner of backgrounds with crew combinations of brother and sister, husband and wife, father and son, father and daughter, friends and all female teams. No matter what the combination Zapcatters have a passion for life and a need for speed!

Although it is a high-performance machine, competing in the Zapcat National Championships is a truly affordable motor sport. A new race-ready Zapcat retails at £7950 including VAT, and with race entry fees of a little over £1,000 for the season, teams can race for approximately £10,000 in the first year including the cost of buying the boat, and for about £2,000 in the second season.

The 2007 Zapcat National Championship season comprises seven Grand Prix, each lasting two days with a championship round on each day. The boats race in small packs of up to twelve boats over 16 or 20 heats depending on the venue. Championship points are accumulated in much the same style as the Formula 1 Championship and the team with the most points at the end of the season is crowned champion.

Class 1 and P1

These are the giants of the offshore racing world, with boats traveling up to 160mph and more, and powers up to 1800hp, three times that of a Formula One car. Class 1 are the largest and fastest, with the boat specially designed for racing. P1 has two classes, Evolution, with purpose-designed boats, and speeds up to 125mph, and Supersport, where the boats are production sportscruisers, with maximum speeds of 85mph. They race in series which move round the world, but sadly do not touch down in the UK these days, preferring more exotic locations. The nearest we get is the annual Cowes-Torquay-Cowes race, on August Bank Holiday, which attracts a mixture of racing classes, and the Round Britain Powerboat Race, a gruelling endurance event, last raced in 2008, and before that in 1984 and 1969, but set to make another comeback in 2012. www.class-1.com, www.powerboatp1.com britishpowerboatracingclub. co.uk, rb12.com and www. roundbritainrace.co.uk, are the sites to give you all the information.

Circuit racing

Inland circuit-racing takes place on freshwater lakes and reservoirs. There are many classes, increasing in power and speed, plus junior classes. This is low cost racing, with secondhand rigs changing hands for £500 upwards, but it is nonetheless exciting, with the hydroplanes reaching close to 100mph. Several clubs serve as venues for this sport, one of the longest established and most successful being the Lowestoft and Otlton Broad Motor Boat Club in Suffolk. www.lobmbc.com

John Cooke runs Banana Shark Racing in Devon, specialising in high-performance offshore powerboats for leisure use or racing. www. bananasharkracing.co.uk

Get on the water...
With leading brands you can trust

Whether you are an experienced leisure boater or you are looking to get on the water for the first time, Barrus has an extensive range of boats, engines and accessories from some of the leading marine brands. Our products are available from an extensive network of authorised marine dealers offering professional sales and technical after-sales support.

Visit our website **www.barrus.co.uk** for information on all our marine brands and details of your local dealer.

The Power Behind The Brands
E. P. Barrus Ltd., Launton Road, Bicester, Oxfordshire, OX26 4UR Tel: 01869 326403

Polishing the hull will not only maintain its appearance, it will protect the GRP from salt-water spray, and ultra-violet sunlight, which will damage the gelcoat and cause it to fade

Chapter 14:
Maintenance

Looking after your boat, engine and trailer will not only ensure trouble-free boating throughout the season, it will prevent costly breakdowns and repairs, and enhance their value when you come to sell them. Peter Caplen guides you through the jobs you can tackle yourself

If you are to enjoy trouble-free boating, your craft and its engine will need proper servicing and maintenance through the season, and at the end of the year. Modern engines and equipment are very reliable, but they still have to be looked after. The best time to perform the annual service is at the end of the season so that the engine has the maximum protection to see it through the long, cold winter lay-up period.

Today's engines are sophisticated pieces of engineering, and they should be serviced by a specialist, but there is still plenty of maintenance work you can do yourself around the boat and trailer. The advantage of doing some of this yourself is that you will familiarise yourself with the workings of the boat with the result that there is more chance of being able to correct minor problems which may occur while out on the water.

Annual maintenance

All four-stroke engines require an oil change at least every year, or more frequently if you have put a lot of hours on it. And don't think that if the boat wasn't used much during the season there is no need to change the oil. In a marine engine the oil does far more than just lubricate the moving parts, as it must also protect the inside of the engine from the effects of the corrosive sea air.

The best time to do this is to drain and refill with fresh oil at the end of the season, as the new oil contains fresh anti-corrosion additives to replace those that have been burned up in the old oil. Run the engine for a short while after the new oil has been added and it will coat all the internal surfaces with fresh protection. Oil filters should be changed

Far left:
Pic 1: Changing the engine oil.

Pic 2: Changing outboard gear oil

Pic 3: Changing inboard oil filters

Pic 4: If your outboard has been used in the sea, it should be flushed with fresh water using a hose and muff clamped over the cooling intakes. Do this at the end of every season as a minimum, or even better after every use in the sea

Pic 5: Changing inboard fuel filters

Pic 6: Checking the spark-plug gaps

t the same time to ensure that ast season's impurities are emoved along with the old ilter cartridge.

Outboard motor gearbox nd outdrive oils must also e changed annually as the ondition of the oil is a good ndication of whether water has ntered the gearbox through he shaft seals. If water is found n the oil (which will then have sludgy, milky appearance) hen the source of the leak nust be found before fresh oil s put in. For inboard engines earbox oil only needs topping up annually and should not need changing more than every two years.

The cooling water system needs attention to ensure it is clear of obstructions. Whether it is an inboard or outboard, flushing the cooling water system with fresh water will also help to cut down on internal corrosion. Flushing an outboard motor cooling system using a hose clamped to the intakes, or better still in bath of fresh water is easy to do.

Flushing an inboard engine's system is less easy, requiring water to be poured through the raw-water side of the circuit. It is also important to drain the raw-water side to prevent freezing, or introduce anti-freeze, which will prevent the rubber impeller being damaged. Outboard motor cooling systems automatically drain down after flushing so this is not a problem, though it is important to let all the water drain out before tilting the leg, in case some water remains trapped.

The secret of reliable engine operation is always clean fuel, so it is important to change the fuel filters during the end of season service and also to discard old petrol so that it doesn't gum-up the carburettors during the lay-up period. With four-strokes the easiest method is to put the old fuel into the car, while two-stroke mixture can be taken home to put it in your strimmer for example.

Diesel fuel does not deteriorate in the same way as petrol so in this case the best practice is to top the fuel tank up to the brim to prevent condensation forming within the tank. This also means you get next year's fuel at last year's prices! If you are running on summer grade diesel, it may not have anti-freeze additive in it. Check with your marina, and if necessary add a can to prevent it going waxy in the cold.

Other more familiar service jobs are cleaning or changing the spark plugs, along with air filter replacement. Air filters usually last longer in boats than in road vehicles as they are not subject to the dust and pollution that car filters have to contend with so it will probably be OK to change them every two years or 100 hours.

Items more specific to marine engines are the water pump impellers. For best practice these should be removed from the pump and stored in a warm dry place through the winter. Failure to do this can lead to them becoming brittle and distorted which often

Pic 7: Remove inboard water pump impellers for winter storage

Pic 8: Check and remove pump and alternator belts for winter storage

Pic 9: Pull the starter-cord out fully and check for fraying or wear

Pic 10: Grease all lubrication points on outboard motors

Pic 11: Check and top up hydraulic steering levels

Pic 12: Check propeller condition and send for repair if necessary

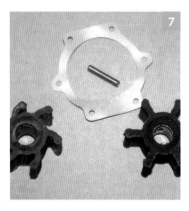

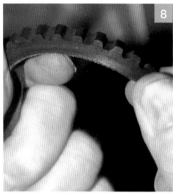

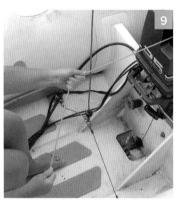

causes early breakage at the start of the new season. The same applies to drive belts and alternator belts which suffer from hardening when left in the same position in a freezing atmosphere.

The pull-cord on manual start outboards will wear in time, and it is good practice to carefully pull it out as far as it will go and with someone holding it out against the spring to examine the entire length. If it is found to be worn or frayed then it should be replaced.

The trim and tilt mechanisms on large outboards and outdrives needs checking for correct operation and the hydraulic system levels topping up as required. The pivot points usually have at least one grease point and this should be greased using water-resistant grease. The same applies to the steering swivel which will need greasing to ensure the steering remains smooth and free.

The whole steering system will appreciate greasing, and all connections should be checked for tightness. Play in the steering is a sign of wear, and if excessive may require replacement of the steering cable. Hydraulic systems should not suffer from play but if they begin to feel 'spongy' there may be air in the system that needs to be bled out. This may also mean that a leak has developed somewhere in the system that needs to be found and rectified. Similarly if the hydraulic fluid level needs regular topping up this is another indication of a leak.

The propeller is the final link in the drive between the engine and the water and its condition will decide how well the boat

performs. It is therefore well worth checking its condition and if found to be chipped or bent, having it professionally repaired and balanced.

Electrics

With the engine serviced and ready for winter it is time to turn to the electrics, starting with the batteries. If the boat has traditional batteries then first check the electrolyte level and if any levels are low, top up with de-ionised water. Clean any corrosion off the terminals and coat with either Vaseline or anti-corrosive grease.

Moving on to the starter motor and alternator, make sure all the connections are tight and corrosion free, if necessary repeating the treatment used on the battery terminals. If the boat has fuses rather than circuit breakers, it is worth removing each fuse in turn and wiping the connections with a very light smear of anti-corrosive grease before refitting.

External bulbs in the navigation lights, searchlight and cockpit lights will all appreciate similar treatment to ensure they maintain good contact throughout the next season. Treat the plug connectors of cockpit instruments such as depth sounders in the same way. For security's sake it is often worth taking such easily removed items home for safe keeping.

Check the operation of the bilge pump and clean any debris from around the pump inlet. If a float switch is fitted check the operation to ensure it is switching the bilge pump on and off.

Covers

Many smaller boats will have fitted covers to keep the weather out through the winter, but it is important to check these periodically to ensure they have not come undone during windy weather as the fasteners will damage the gel-coat if allowed to flap around in the wind.
Similarly it is not a good idea to use a tarpaulin over the boat. However well it is roped down it will still move about

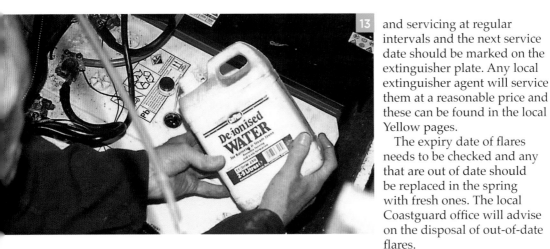

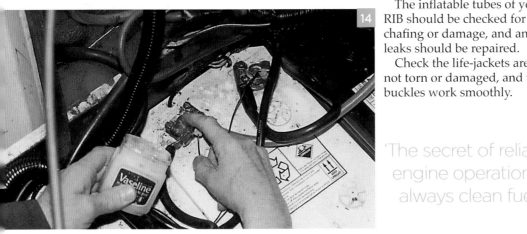

and servicing at regular intervals and the next service date should be marked on the extinguisher plate. Any local extinguisher agent will service them at a reasonable price and these can be found in the local Yellow pages.

The expiry date of flares needs to be checked and any that are out of date should be replaced in the spring with fresh ones. The local Coastguard office will advise on the disposal of out-of-date flares.

The inflatable tubes of your RIB should be checked for chafing or damage, and any leaks should be repaired.

Check the life-jackets are not torn or damaged, and the buckles work smoothly.

'The secret of reliable engine operation is always clean fuel"

Trailer

Don't forget the trailer. This is a road vehicle and carries one of your most expensive possessions, so it is vital to ensure that it is roadworthy and safe. The biggest problem with trailers are the wheel bearings, which corrode when the trailer is regularly immersed for launching and retrieving the boat. Ideally the bearings should be re-greased after every immersion to force out water that has entered and to ensure proper lubrication. I used to do this and although it was messy, I never suffered a wheel bearing failure. Alternatively re-grease once a month and you should have no problems. Check the condition of the wheel bearings as part of the annual service and change them if they look rusty, or sound rough when spun by hand.

Trailer lighting boards, are notoriously unreliable unless looked after. The first sign of problems is when different lights start working dimmed when others are being used. For example, when the indicators are used the brake

n the wind and this will cause chafe on the corners of the superstructure and anywhere else it may rub.

To protect the gel-coat of the hull and maintain its shine you should treat the entire outside of the boat with a good quality wax polish at the end of the season and repeat the treatment in the Spring. Some owners apply a coat of wax n the autumn and then don't polish it off until spring.

The question of anti-fouling he hull will depend on whether the boat is kept afloat hroughout the summer or

whether it normally lives on a trailer. If it stays afloat, anti-fouling is essential to keep the bottom clean and free from weed and barnacle growth. Failing to do this will result in a significant loss of performance plus higher fuel bills. Normally anti-fouling is best applied in the spring a couple of weeks before launching, so it is fresh for the season.

Safety equipment

Safety equipment will need checking at the end of the season. Fire extinguishers need checking for pressure,

Pic 16: Anti-foul each spring if the boat remains afloat throughout the season

Pic 17: Check the fire-extinguishers and have them serviced if required

Pic 18: Check that all flares are in date

Pic 19: Check wheel bearings for wear and replace when worn

Pic 20: Check the outboard motor water circulation tell-tale

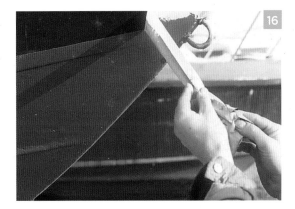

lights also flash dimly, or the side lights dim when the brake lights come on. These problems can almost always be traced to earth faults and can be rectified by cleaning and lightly greasing all the earth connections both on the trailer-board and the connections on the tow vehicle where the trailer socket is earthed.

Trailer brakes need adjusting annually and if they seem to be working less well then the brake shoes should be checked and changed if worn out. When the trailer is stored it is good practice to chock the wheels and leave the handbrake in the off position as this prevents brake cables stretching and shoes sticking to the drums.

If you are in any doubt as to your capability to service the trailer, it should be taken to a specialist every year.

Regular maintenance
The most obvious piece of regular maintenance is a good hose down after every use, especially when used in salt water. Once a month give the boat a wash with shampoo and every three months apply a fresh coat of wax polish. Check the engine oil level before every use, and on two-strokes with oil injection remember to check the level in the oil tank before setting off. Also check the fuel level before setting off. Running out of fuel at sea is the height of stupidity and will put you and your passengers into danger, so don't let it happen to you.

Always check that the cooling water is circulating through the engine before setting off. With outboards you should see a good stream from the tell-tale, while on a sterndrive you should watch the temperature gauge.

Check the condition of the propeller regularly through the season.

Use a clean funnel with a fine filter when filling the outboard tank to ensure the petrol is clean and sediment-free.

Check and grease the trailer wheel bearings at regular intervals. Check the trailer lighting board before every trip.

If you have doubts about your ability to perform any of the maintenance jobs described here then get them done professionally, remember that the welfare state ends at the sea wall and breakdowns at sea are far more hazardous than a breakdown on the motorway! That said, go out and enjoy your boating knowing that your craft is well maintained and up to scratch.

Eagle 645 Luxury Sports Rib

BRIG
inflatable boats

Eagle Range (cm): 340, 380, 500, 580, 645, 780

Outboard Directory

If you need spares or service when you are away from home, or if you are thinking of travelling to a new area, and want to ring ahead for some local information or advice, give the nearest dealer a call. We will be updating the list regularly on our Getting Afloat website, **www.gettingafloat.co.uk.**

HONDA
www.honda.co.uk
Tel: 0845 200 8000

ENGLAND
AC Outboards
Market Deeping, Cambs
01780 480169

Ely Boat Chands
Ely, Cambs
01353 663095

Fox Marine
Jersey, CI
01534 721312

Herm Seaway
Guernsey, CI
01481 726829

Midway Boats
Nantwich, Cheshire
01270 528482

Challenger Marine
Penryn, Cornwall
01326 377222

Henry Armer & Son
Ulverston, Cumbria
01229 820877

John Bridger Marine
Exeter, Devon
01392 216420

Tony Hole Marine
Plymouth, Devon
01752 407070

Mullacott Caravans & Marine
Ilfracombe, Devon
01271 863066

Rob Perry Marine
Axminster, Devon
01297 631314

SMS (Salcombe)
Salcombe, Devon
01548 843655

SMS (Plymouth)
Plymouth, Devon
01752 666333

Tonto Marine
Galmpton, Devon
01803 844399

Poole Marine
Poole, Dorset
01202 679577

Eastern Leisure
Wallasea Island, Essex
01702 257090

L.H. Morgan
Colchester, Essex
01206 302003

Powersport Ltd
Manchester
0161 6834978

Auto Marine
Southsea, Hants
02392 825601

C- Power Marine
Warsash, Hants
01489 559555

M B Marine
Southampton, Hants
02380 388608

Pacer Marine
Aldershot, Hants
01252 317100

S A L Marine
Lymington, Hants
01590 679588

Yachthaven Marine
Ballasalla, IOM
01624 822 995

Cheetah Marine
Ventnor, IOW
01983 852398

RHP Marine
Cowes, IOW
01983 200 035

G & M Motors
Gravesend, Kent
01474 365026

Portguide
Maidstone, Kent
01622 817570

Bridgehouse Marina
Nateby, Lancs
01995 607690

Raider Boats
Carnforth, Lancs
01524 823963

Raider Boats
Nether Kellett, Lancs
01524 823 963

Warrior Boats
Preston, Lancs
01772 459666

Chiswick Honda
Chiswick, London
0208 9968100

Bridgehouse Marina
Nr Garstang, Lancs
01995 607690

Liverpool Powerboats
Liverpool, Merseyside
0151 944 1163

P F K Ling
Harleston, Norfolk
01379 853495

Marine Tech
S Walsham, Norfolk
01603 270058

British Waterways
Sawley, Notts
0115 972 5471

S R Boats
Misterton, Notts
01427 891144

Red Line Outboards
Abingdon, Oxon
01235 521562

Maestermyn Marine
Oswestry, Shropshire
01691 662424

Advance Marine
Bristol, Somerset
01275 815910

Ribcraft Ltd
Yeovil, Somerset
01935 411846

Stone Boats
Stone, Staffs
01785 812688

P F K Ling
Lowestoft, Suffolk
01502 537444

Seamark Nunn
Felixstowe, Suffolk
01394 451000

Shetland Boats
Bury St Eds, Suffolk
01359 235 255

D & R Engineering
Walton, Surrey
01932 254180

Trident UK
Gateshead, Tyne /Wear
0191 4901736

T L Harvey
Wednesbury, W Midlands
0121 568 8837

Mailspeed Marine
Crawley Down, W Sussex
01342 713524

Marine Performance
Upton on Severn, Worcs
01684 594 540

Methley Bridge Chands
Castleford, Yorks
01977 735400

Humber Fabrications
Hull, Yorks
01482 226100

Viking Marine
Goole, Yorks
01405 765737

SCOTLAND
Mackay Marine
Aberdeen
01224 575772

Ardoran Marine
Oban
01631 566123

Robertsons of Tain
Wick
01955 602296

Arisaig Marine
Arisaig
01687 450224

Gael Force Marine
Inverness
01463 229400

Clyde Outboards
Gourock
01475 635700

Production Yachts
S Queensferry
0131 331 4496

Robertsons of Tain
Tain
01862 892276

J & W Tait
Kirkwall
01856 873 003

Thulecraft
Lerwick, Shetland
01595 693192

WALES
Yachtshop
Holyhead
01407 760031

Network N Wales
Conwy
01492 580001

Pembrokeshire Yachts
Milford Haven
01646 602030

Wigmore Wright
Penarth
02920 709983

Robert Owen Marine
Portmadoc
01766 513435

Young's Boats
Swansea
01792 480490

IRELAND
Aquashak
Carrickfergus
028 9332 6304

John K Cathcart
Enniskillen
028 6632 4325

Red Bay Boats
Cushendall
028 2177 1331

Sands Marine
Lurgan
028 3834 3911

MARINER
EP Barrus.
www.barrus.co.uk
Tel: 01869 363613

ENGLAND
Bristol Boats
Bristol, Avon
01225 872032

Priory Marine
Bedford, Beds
01234 330592

Drive Line Marine
Reading, Berks
01189 423877

A C Outboards
Peterborough, Cambs
01780 480169

G B Watersports
Peterborough, Cambs
01733 322108

Hartford Marina
Huntingdon, Cambs
01480 454677

Riverside Marine
St Ives, Cambs
01480 468666

G T Marine 2000
Jersey, CI
01534 721702

Bill Higham
Manchester, Cheshire
0161 7907678

CTC Marine
Middsbro, Cleveland
01642 230123

CTC Marine
Billingham, Cleveland
01542 372600

Boating World
Saltash, Cornwall
01752 851679

Falmouth Yachts
Falmouth, Cornwall
01326 370060

Outboard Services
Lostwithiel, Cornwall
01208 873515

Rock Marine
Wadebridge, Cornwall
01208 863396

Lakeland Electric Boat
Penrith, Cumbria
01768 840211

Windermere Aquatic
Bowness, Cumbria
01539 442121

Mayday Marine
Chesterfield, Derbys
01246 453645

Rob Perry Marine
Axminster, Devon
01297 631314

John Bridger
Exeter, Devon
01392 216420

Birchell Marine
Paignton, Devon
01803 522146

Marine Boat Sales
Paignton, Devon
01803 834004

Mount Batten Boats
Plymouth, Devon
01752 482666

Quarterdeck Marine
Plymouth, Devon
01752 224567

Blue Water Marine
Salcombe, Devon
01548 843383

RIBS Marine
Christchurch, Dorset
01202 477327

Rockley Watersports
Poole, Dorset
01202 677272

Holes Bay Marine
Poole, Dorset
01202 66720

Salterns Marina
Poole, Dorset
01202 707391

Select Marine
Poole, Dorset
01202 742474

Service N Repair
Colchester, Essex
01206 385008

Viking Mouldings
Gt Dunmow, Essex
01371 875214

Boating Mania
Upminster, Essex
01708 223065

L H Morgan
Brightlingsea, Essex
01206 302003

Service n Repair
W.Mersea, Essex
01206 385008

Samspeed Marine
Falfield, Glos
01454 260123

Force 4 Chandlery
Nailsworth, Glos
0845 1300710

Aluminium Boats
Hayling Island, Hants
023 9246 1968

Trevor Hobbs
Botley, Hants
01489 785009

Burseldon Outboards
Bursledon, Hants
02380 406648

Home Marine
Emsworth, Hants
01243 374125

Dave Crawford
Lymington, Hants
01590 671251

Extreme Marine
Southampton, Hants
02380 639278

Fairweather Marine
Fareham, Hants
01329 283500

Pacer Marine
Aldershot, Hants
01252 317100

Yachthaven Marine
Ballasalla, IOM
01624 822995

Gemstar Assoc
Yarmouth, IOW
01983 760521

IOW Outboards
Yarmouth, IOW
01983 760521

Danson Park Marine
Sidcup, Kent
0208 304 5678

Highway Marine
Sandwich, Kent
01304 614814

Portguide Marine
Wateringbury, Kent
01622 817570

ower Products
trood, Kent
1634 711267

oat & Outboard
entre
Garstang, Lancs
1995 607690

ouglas Marine
reston, Lancs
1772 812462

R Harris & Son
eicester, Leics
1162 692135

J Marine
ew Holland,
eics
1469 532231

portique Ski
oats
outh, Lincs
1472 388296

Chas Newens
utney, London
20 8788 4587

indon Lewis
hepperton,
Middx
1932 254844

Gorleston Marine
orleston, Norfolk
1493 661883

Harbour
Chandlery
Well-next-Sea,
Norfolk
1328 710676

Marine Tech
Walsham,
Norfolk
1603 270058

A Lynch
Morpeth,
Northumbs
1670 512291

incolnshire M/S
ast Bridgford,
Notts
1949 21122

Newark Marina
ewark, Notts
1636 704022

ed Line
Outboards
Abingdon,
Oxfordshire
1235 521562

eamark Nunn
elixstowe,
uffolk
1394 451000

Orkney Boats
rundel, Sussex
1243 551456

Oakley Motor
Units
Brighton, Sussex
1273 603322

MS Marine
Chichester, Sussex
1243 542632

Ribs & Outboards
U
chenor, Sussex
1243 512374

aquatec Marine
ancing, Sussex
1903 762610

Boat Exhibitions
Newhaven, Sussex
01273 612612

A Pace Eng
Newhaven, Sussex
01273 516010

Powerboat Sales
Southam, Warks
01327264367

Avon Boating
Stratford, Warks
01789 269977

Hedley of Halifax
Halifax, Yorkshire
01422 362355

York Marina
York, Yorkshire
01904 621021

York Marina
York, Yorkshire
01904 704442

SCOTLAND
Fettes & Rankine
Aberdeen
01224 573343

**Ardfern Yacht
Cent**
Argyll
01852 500247

J N MacDonald
Glasgow
0141 810 3400

**The Outboard
Shop**
Largs
01475 560324

Keil Engines
Oban
01631 720380

Bosun's Locker
Edinburgh
0131 331 3875

**Forth Yacht
Marina**
Edinburgh
0131 331 3875

Arran Boat Sales
Crieff
01764 685376

Kip Marina
Renfrewshire
01475 521485

Ian Irvine Eng
Whalsay, Shetland
Is
01806 566627

Sea & Shore
Dundee, Tayside
01382 450666

WALES
Dulas Boats
Dulas
01248 410266

Conwy Marine
Conwy
01492 58001

Blue Marine
Cardigan
01239 810484

Shaddow Marine
Swansea
07771 868745

Wigmore Wright
Cardiff
029 20709983

Glaslyn Marine
Porthmadog
01766 513545

Llyn Marine
Pwllheli
01758 612606

Ian Williams
Pwllheli
01758 720472

M Jones Marine
Kilgetty
01834 891237

**West Wales
Yahama**
Neyland
01646 602288

IRELAND
Preston Marine
Bangor
02891 461458

Motor Marine
Burtonport
00353 749542277

O B Marine
Dublin
00353 1834 1855

Derg Marina
Co Clare
00353 61376364

Marine Eng
Munster
Co Cork
00353 214701667

**North South
Marine**
Lisnaskea
02867 721720

Sands Marine
Lurgan
02838 343911

**West Coast
Marine**
Co Mayo
00353 96 78630

Sheelin Boats
Mountnugent
00353 49854
0101

Sirius Marine
Waterford
00353 51 595000

MERCURY
EP Barrus.
www.barrus.co.uk
Tel: 01869 363613

ENGLAND
Advance Marine
Bristol, Avon
01275 815910

**Walker
Outboards**
Reading,
Berkshire
0118 947 8641

Gallichan Marine
Jersey, CI
01534 746387

Offshore Power
Guernsey, CI
01481 247048

Northwich Marina
Northwich,
Cheshire
01606 44475

Shipshape Marine
Stockport,
Cheshire
0161 483 0666

Black Dog Marine
East Looe,
Cornwall
01503 265898

Robin Curnow
Penryn, Cornwall
01326 373438

Shepherds Marine
Bowness,
Cumbria
01539 446004

Ullswater Marine
Watermillock,
Cumbs
01768 486415

Ribquest
Dronfield, Derbys
01246 411366

Central Marine
Ilkeston, Derbys
01159 442442

Ash Marine
Exeter, Devon
01392 876654

**Blue Water
Marine**
Salcombe, Devon
01548 843383

Mariners Weigh
Teignmouth,
Devon
01626 873698

Mobile Marine
Axminster, Devon
01297 631821

Tonto Marine
Galmpton, Devon
01803 844399

Tony Hole Marine
Plymouth, Devon
01752 407070

Wills Marine
Kingsbridge,
Devon
01548 852424

**Mobile Marine
Eng**
Lyme Regis,
Dorset
01297 631821

Dorset Yacht
Poole, Dorset
01202 674531

Marinautic
Poole, Dorset
01202 678 085

Yellow Penguin
Poole, Dorset
01202 710448

Kingfisher Marine
Weymouth,
Dorset
01305 766595

**E Counties
Leisure**
Wallesea Island,
Essex
01702 257090

French Marine
Brightlingsea,
Essex
01206 305233

Frinton Boats
Frinton on Sea,
Essex
01255 850440

**Walkers Yacht
Chand**
Leigh on Sea,
Essex
01702 421321

**Doug Ashley
Marine**
Nazeing, Essex
01992 892259

A & D Marine
Gloucester, Glos
01452 415430

Map Marine
Andover, Hants
01264 889043

**Russell
Powerboats**
Basingstoke,
Hants
01252 877337

Home Marine
Emsworth, Hants
01243 374125

**Sea
Teach**
Emsworth, Hants
01329 283500

**Solent
Ribs**
Fareham, Hants
01329 283500

BHG Marine
Lymington, Hants
0845 6446645

Dave Crawford
Lymington, Hants
01590 671251

Ron Hale Marine
Portsmouth,
Hants
023 92732985

**Hunton
Powerboats**
Romsey, Hants
01794 515236

**BBMS
(Swanwick)**
Southampton,
Hants
01489 580250

M.B. Marine
Southampton,
Hants
02380 388608

Marina Marbella
Southampton,
Hants
023 8045 3005

Barnet Marine
Welwyn G City,
Herts
01707 331389

Bryher Marine
Bryher, Isle of
Scilly
01720 423047

**Bembridge
Marine**
Bembridge, IOW
01983 872817

Wayne Maddox
Margate, Kent
01843 297157

**Whitstable
Marine**
Whitstable, Kent
01227 274168

**Liverpool
Powerboats**
Bootle, Lancs
0151 944 1163

Raider Boats
Carnforth, Lancs
0771 0006881

**Outboard &
Hydroplane**
Nr Ormskirk,
Lancs
01695 422350

Douglas Marine
Preston, Lancs
01772 812462

Rib-X
Leicester, Leics
0116 277 7373

**Burton Waters
Marina**
Lincoln, Lincs
01522 567404

Lindon Lewis
Shepperton,
Middx
01932 254844

Norfolk Marine
Wroxham, Norfolk
01603 783150

Amble Boats
Amble,
Northumbs
01665 710267

Beeston Marina
Beeston, Notts
01159 223168

**Shrewsbury
Marine**
Shrewsbury,
Shrops
01743 242555

D B Marine
Taunton,
Somerset
01823 272222

Emtec UK
Stoke, Staffs
01782 787989

C C Marine
Beccles, Suffolk
01502 713703

Seapower Marine
Ipswich, Suffolk
01473 780090

**Kings
Marine**
Chertsey, Surrey
01932 564830

IMS Marine
Aldingbourne,
Sussex
01243 542632

**Oakley
Motors**
Brighton, Sussex
01273 603322

West Marine
Brighton, Sussex
01273 626656

Adrian Cronk
Chichester,
Sussex
01243 542046

Tate & Crew
Eastbourne,
Sussex
01323 479000

A Pace Marine
Newhaven,
Sussex
01273 516010

**Peter Leonard
Marine**
Newhaven,
Sussex
01273 515987

Storra Marine
Newcastle, Tyne/
Wear
0191 266 1037

Meridian Marine
Sutton Coldfield,
W Mids
0121 323 2333

T L Harvey
Darlaston, W Mids
0121 5688837

**Fletcher
Boats**
Wolverhampton,
W Mids
0845 2305670

**Wakering
Eng**
Evesham,
Worc
01386 768500

**Marine
Performance**
Upton Severn,
Worcs
01684 594540

**Scarborough
Marine**
Scarborough,
Yorks
01723 375199

SCOTLAND
**Buccaneer
Marine**
Aberdeenshire
01261 835199

Fettes & Rankine
Aberdeen
0224 573343

Keil Engine Serv
Argyll
01631 720380

Swordfish Marine
Dunoon
01369 701905

**Upper Largo
Chandlery**
Fife
01333 360217

**Caley
Cruisers**
Inverness
01463 236539

DDZ Marine
Largs
01475 686072

Kippford Slipway
Kippford
01556 620249

Edward Crossan
Balloch
01389 754363

Ferry Marine
S Queensferry
0131 331 1233

Upper Largo Chands
Leven
01333 360217

Findhorn Marina
Findhorn
01309 690099

Mitchell Outboards
Renfrew
0141 886 4222

D H Marine
Lerwick
01595 690618

WALES
M.E.S Marine
Flintshire
01244 289977

Anglesey Boats
Beaumaris
01248 811413

Gower Marine
Burry Port
01792 390602

Aberscoch Land /Sea
Pwllheli
01758 713434

Blue Water Marine
Pwllheli
01758 614600

Harbour Marine
Pwllheli
01758 701707

Robert Owen Marine
Porthmadog
01766 513435

Dale Sailing
Milford Haven
01646 603110

Robust Boats
Haverfordwest
01437 720089

Acadia Marine
Glamorgan
01792 459299

West Point Marine
Cardiff
029 2037 3400

Youngs Boatyard
Swansea
01792 480490

IRELAND
M G Stitt
Larne
02893 382278

John Mcaleese
Scarva
02838 831617

O'Malley Marine
Sixmilebridge
0035361 369342

Atlantic Boating
Skibbereen,
00353 2822145

Oysterhaven Boats Co
Cork
00353 21 4843626

Marine Motors
Cork
00353 2143 54217

Gulfstream Marine
Derry,
028 7136 8779

Spinnaker Marine
Dun Laoghaire
00353 1280 6654

Preston Marine
Bangor
02891 461458

Robert Dickie
Enniskillen, Co Fermanagh
00353 28 6632 2155

SUZUKI
www.suzuki-marine.
co.uk
Tel: 0500 011959

ENGLAND
Priory Marine
Bedford, Beds
01234 330592

D K Collins
Jersey, CI
01534 732415

Shoreline Marine
Guernsey, CI
01481 255975

Nationwide Marine
Warrington, Cheshire
01925 245788

Mylor Yacht Harbour
Falmouth, Cornwall
01326 376588

Outboard Services
Lostwithiel, Cornwall
01298 873515

Rock Marine
Wadebridge, Cornwall
01208 863396

South'ard Eng
St Mary's, Cornwall
01720 422539

Nichol End Marine
Keswick, Cumbria
01768 773082

Central Marine
Ilkeston, Derbys
0115 9442442

D2 Marine
Torquay, Devon
01803 897222

Mobile Marine
Axminster, Devon
01297 631821

Promarine UK
Plymouth, Devon
01752 267984

Reddish Marine
Salcombe, Devon
01548 844094

Yachts of Dartmouth
Dartmouth, Devon
01803 833500

Mermaid Marine
Poole, Dorset
01202 677776

Yellow Penguin
Poole, Dorset
01202 710448

Tate & Crewe
Eastbourne
E Sussex
01323 479000

Boating Mania
Upminster,
Essex
01708 226909

Brightlingsea Boats
Brightlingsea, Essex
01206 304747

Powersport
Manchester
0161 6834978

Fairweather Marine
Fareham, Hants
01329 283500

Home Marine
Emsworth, Hants
01243 374125

M B Marine
Southampton, Hants
023 80388608

Pacer Marine
Aldershot, Hants
01252 317100

Ron Hale Marine
Portsmouth, Hants
023 92732985

S A L Marine
Lymington, Hants
01590 679588

Warsash Marine
Southampton, Hants
01489 579860
Yachthaven

Marine
Ballasalla,
I of Man
01624 822995

Kevin Mole O/Bs
Cowes, IOW
01983 289699

Gillingham Marina
Gillingham, Kent
01634 283008

Whitstable Marine
Whistable, Kent
01227 262 525

Warrior Boats
Preston, Lancs
01772 459666

L R Harris
Syston, Leics
0116 2692135

National A1 Marine
Upton, Merseyside
01519 098067

Bridge Marine
Shepperton, Middx
01932 245126

Doug Ashley
St Olaves, Norfolk
01493 488000

Marinepower
Brundall, Norfolk
01603 717525

Standard House Chands
Wells next Sea, Norfolk
01328 710593

P A Lynch
Morpeth, Northumbs
01670 512291

Advance Marine
Bristol, Somerset
01275 815910

Ribcraft
Yeovil, Somerset
01935 411846

Marine Tec
Stoke, Staffs
01782 787989

BCT
Mildenhall, Suffolk
01638 716220

Seamark Nunn
Felixstowe, Suffolk
01394 451000

Winsor Marine
Camberley, Surrey
01276 683822

T L Harvey
Darlaston, W Mids
0121 5688837

Aquatec Marine
Lancing W Sussex
01903 762610

Mailspeed Marine
Crawley, W Sussex
01342 713524

Ribs & Outboards 4U
Chichester, W Sussex
01243 513020

International Marine
Misterton, Yorks
01427 891144

Pennine Marine
Skipton, Yorks
01756 792335

York Marine
York, Yorks
01904 704442

SCOTLAND
Mackay Marine
Aberdeen
01224 575772

Silvers Marine
Helensburgh
01436 831 222

C J Marine
Galston
01292 313400

DDZ Marine
Largs
01475 686072

Bosuns Locker
South Queensferry
0131 3313875

David Anderson
Newport on Tay
01382 541848

Gael Force Marine
Inverness
01463 229400

Ardoran Marine
Argyll
01631 566123

Duncan Yacht Chand
Glasgow
0141 4296044

Loch Lomond Marina
Alexandria
01389 752069

Harris Marine
Harris
01859 502221

Orkney Tool Hire
Kirkwall
01856 870000

Garriock Bros
Lerwick
01595 694765

WALES
Yachtshop
Holyhead
01407 760031

Dale Sailing
Milford Haven
01646 603110

Dickies at Pwllheli
Pwllheli
01758 701828

Dickies at Bangor
Bangor
01248 363411

Harbour Marine
Pwllheli
01758 701707

Cambrian Boat Cent
Swansea,
01792 467263

Goodwick Marine
Goodwick,
01348 874590

IRELAND
Gulfstream Marine
Derry
02871 368779

North Atlantic Ribs
Derry City
028 71362304

Outboard Services
Down Patrick
02844 821000

Red Bay Boats
Cushendall
02821 771331

Sands Marine
Armagh
028 38343911

YAMAHA
www.yamaha-motor.
co.uk
Tel: 01932 358000

ENGLAND
ESPAR
Marlow, Bucks
01628 471368

A C Outboards
Market Deeping,
01780 480169

Sunsport Marine
St Sampson, Guernsey
01481 248466

Gallichan Marine
St Aubin, Jersey
01534 746387

Shipshape Marine
Stockport, Cheshire
0161 4830666

Midway Boats
Nantwich, Cheshire
01270 528482

Craven Marine
Exmouth,
01395 269334

Rock Marine
Wadesbridge, Cornwall
01208 863396

G W Doling
Barrow, Cumbria
01229 823708

Maiden Marine
Windermere, Cumbria
01539 488050

Mobile Marine
Axminster, Devon
01297 631821

Chris Hoyle Marine
Dartmouth, Devon
01803 752221

Yeoward & Dowie
Salcombe, Devon
01548 844261

Mechanical Services
Weymouth, Dorset
01305 779379

Salterns Marina
Poole, Dorset
01202 707391

Oakley Motors
Brighton, E Sussex
01273 603322

French Marine
Brightlingsea, Essex
01206 302133

The Boat Shop
Rainham, Essex
01708 523016

Samspeed Marine
Wooton U Edge, Glos
01454 260123

Pacer Marine
Aldershot, Hants
01252 317100

BHG Marine
Lymington, Hants
01590 613600

Ron Hale Marine
Southsea, Hants
02392 732985

Warsash Marine
Warsash, Hants
01489 583813

Barnet Marine
Welwyn G City, Herts
01707 331 389

Bottomline
Douglas, IOM
01624 671671

Outboard Marine
Glen Maye, IOM
01624 845662

Kevin Mole O/Bs
Cowes, IOW
01983 289699

Harwoods
Yarmouth, IOW
01983 760258

Wayne Maddox
Margate, Kent
01843 297157

Power Products
Rochester, Kent
01634 711267

Kings Marine
Chertsey,
01932 564830

Liverpool Powerboats
Bootle, Merseyside
0151 944 1163

Lindon Lewis
Shepperton, Middx
01932 247427

Boston Putford
Lowestoft, Norfolk
01502 565661

E F Snelling
King's Lynn, Norfolk
01485 210381

Marine Tech
S Walsham, Norfolk
01603 270058

Burton Waters
Lincoln, Lincs
01522 567404

E F Snelling
King's Lynn, Norfolk
01485 210381

Marine Tech
S Walsham, Norfolk
01603 270058

Bob Spalding
Ipswich, Suffolk
01473 659674

Lansdale Marine
Birdham, W
Sussex
01243 512374

Storrar Marine
Newcastle U Tyne
0191 266 1037

Avon Boating
Stratford, Warks
01789 269977

Marine
Performance
Upton on Seven,
Worcs
01684 594540

Rodley Boat
Centre
Leeds, Yorks
0113 2576132

Selby Boat
Centre
Selby, Yorks
01757 212211

Pennine Marine
Skipton, Yorks
01756 792335

SCOTLAND
Mackay Marine
Aberdeen
01224 575772

Crinan Boatyard
Lochgilphead
01546 830232

Duncan Yacht
Chands
Glasgow
0141 4296044

Stoddarts of
Oban
Oban, Argyll
01631 564176

Castle Douglas
Eng
Castle Douglas
01556 503365

C J Marine
Glaston,
01292 313400

Yampower
Glasgow,
0141 7785384

Caley Marina
Inverness
01463 233437

David Anderson
Marine
Newport on Tay
01382 541848

The Bosuns
Locker
South
Queensferry
0131 3313875

Thulecraft
Lerwick
01595 693192

Orkney Tool Hire
Kirkwall,
01856 870000

WALES
M Dickie
Bangor
01248 363400

West Point
Marine
Cardiff
02920 373400

Abersoch
Boatyard
Pwllheli
01758 713900

Blue Water
Marine
Pwllheli
01758 614600

Dulas Boats
Dulas
01248 410266

Cambrian Boats
Swansea
01792 467263

W Wales Yamaha
Neyland
01646 602288

IRELAND
Cyril Johnston
Belfast
02890 813121

Hanna Boats
Coleraine
028 27662212

Flood Marine
Omagh
028 82246539

Red Bay Boats
Ballymena
0282 177 1331

Jet Products
Strabane
02881 658668

Atlantic Boating
Skibbereen
00353 28 22145

Landers Leisure
Tralee
00353 66 712
4378

Inland Inflatables
Sligo
00353 71 914 4766

Ivor's
Shantalla
00353 91 587400

KER Services
Killybegs
00353 74 973
1525

OB Marine
Dublin
00353 1 834 1855

O'Connors
Garage
Cong
00353 92 46008

O'Neills
Milltown
00353 66 9767163

Killen Marine
Dublin
00353 1 285 3908

New Ross O/Bs
Wexford
00353 51 421902

Meagher Lake
Boats
Borrisokane
00353 67 27356

East Bros
Boyle
00353 79 62710

Southern
England
B H G Marine
Lymington 01590
613600

Yarmouth Marine
Yarmouth 01983
760521

BVD Marine
Bowcombe 01983
532727

Extreme Marine
Southampton
02380 639278

Fairweather
Marine
Fareham 01329
283500

Force 4
Chandlery
Lymington 01590
673698

Force 4
Chandlery
Poole 01202
723311

Holes Bay Marine
Poole 01202
667202

Pacer Marine
Aldershot 01252
317100

Ski Marine
Bournemouth
01202 512637

Aquatech Eng
Lancing 01903
762610

IMS Marine
Chichester 01243
542632

Rib Shop
Southampton
01489 556803

Dave Crawford
Lymington 01590
671251

Winsor Marine
Camberley 07729
003449

Ivors Eng
Hayling Is 02392
466999

Ron Hale Marine
Portsmouth
02392 732985

South West
Ash Marine
Exeter 01392
876654

Blue Water
Weymouth 01305
782080

Boating World
Landrake
01752 851679

Bristol Boats
Bristol 01225
872032

D B Marine
Honiton 01404
861810

Force 4 Chand
Bristol 01179
268396

John Bridger
Exeter 01392
250970

Marine Bazaar
Plymouth 01752
201003

Peter Dixon
Chand
Exmouth 01395
273248

Reddish Marine
Salcombe, 01548
844094

Samspeed
Marine
Falfield 01454
260123

Seacat Marine
Padstow 01841
520558

Tonto Marine
Galmpton 01803
844399

Mariners Weigh
Shaldon
01626 873698

Outboard
Services
Lostwithiel
01208 873515

Riviera Boats
Torquay
01803 872945

Challenger
Marine
Penryn
01326 377222

Chris Brown
Marine
Ilfracombe
07843 276913

R J Marine
Rooksbridge
01934 750912

Torquay Chand
Torquay
01803 211854

Fowey Harbour
Fowey
01726 832806

Bennett
Boatyard
Bryher
0172042205

Sea-Swift Boats
Kingsteignton
01626 335904

South East
Clydach Marine
Sevenoaks
01732 740843

Force 4 Chand
Chichester
01243 773788

N S Marine
Worthing
01903 507076

A Pace Marine
Newhaven
01273 516010

Sussex Marine
St Leonards
01424 425882

Whitstable
Marine
Whitstable
01227 274168

Rye Harbour
Marine
Rye 01797 227667

Arun Nautique
Littlehampton
01903 730558

Whitton Marine
Rochester
01634 250593

Outboard Spares
Maidstone
01622 817073

LONDON
Barnet Marine
Barnet
01707 331389

Chas Newens
Putney
0208 788 4587

Chertsey Marine
Chertsey
01932 565195

Baudain's Marine
Balham
07813 829043

Adec Marine
Croydon 0208
6869717

Bridge Marine
Shepperton
01932 245126

EAST ANGLIA
A C Outboards
Peterborough
01780 480169

Brightlingsea
Boats
Brightlingsea
01206 304747

Essex Marine
Canvey Island
01268 795554

Boatacs
Westcliff
01702 475057

T S Rigging
Maldon
01621 874861

Antony Kettley
Ipswich
01473 788128

Marine Tech
Norwich
01603 270058

Midlands
D P Marine
Wolverhampton
01902 755951

L R Harris
Leicester
01162 692735

Lincoln Marine
E Bridgford
01949 21122

Redhill Marine
Nottingham
01509 672770

Seamark
Sutton Coldfield
0121 3225335

Topaz Marine
Welford on Avon,
01789 750878

Leisure Boats
Leamington Spa,
0845 45695333

A&D Marine
Gloucester 01452
415430

B S Motorsport
Westcott,
01296 658422

Northern England
Amble Marina
Amble
01665 712168

Bill Higham
Worsley
0161 790 7678

Derwent Water
Keswick
01768 772912

G. W. Dowling
Cumbria
01229 823708

Derek Lowdon
Kendal
01539 733737

Pendle Marine
Preston
01772 691010

M J Marine
New Holland
01469 532231

Shipshape
Marine
Stockport
0161 4830666

Beeston Marine
Nottingham
0115 9678482

Farebrother
Marine
Chester
01244 332633

Hartlepool
Marine
Hartlepool
01429 862932

Liverpool
Powerboats
Liverpool 0
151 9441163

Boroughbridge
Marina
York
01423 323400

Pennant Marine
Jarrow 0191
4894686

Boat & O/B
Centre
Garstang,
01995 607690

Velocity Marine
North Ferriby
01482 632137

Jacksons Marine
Cumbria
01946 599332

Rovogate
Pontefract
01977 796472

St Patricks Boats
Penrith
01768 482393

Pennine Marine
Skipton
01756 792335

Sea Hunter
Boats
Blackpool 01253
352707

Powerboats R us
Sheffield
01142 611222

Scotland
Ardwell Marine
Stranraer
01776 860297

Gael Force
Inverness
01463 229400

Harris Marine
Harris
01859 502221

Ian Irvine
Shetland
01806 566627

Isle of Sky
Yachts
Ardvasar
01471 844216

Keil Engines
Oban
01631 720380

Mitchell
Outboards
Renfrew
0141 8864222

Stornoway
Spares
Isle of Lewis
01851 702504

Highlander
Boats
Tayport
01382 553111

Yampower
Glasgow 0141
7785384

Clyde Outboard
Gourock
01475 635700

Plant & Marine
Kirkibost
01851 612476

Outboard Shop
Fairlie
01475 560324

Kippford Slipway
Kippford
01556 620249

Marin Subsea
Ellon
01358 722526

Propell Marine
Elgin
07565947778

Arran Boat Sales
St Fillans
01764 685376

WALES
Blue Marine
Cardigan
01239 814600

Dulas Boats
Anglesey
01248 410266

Greenwell Marine
Carmarthen
01554 771056

Harbour Marine
Pwllheli
01758 701707

Marine Scene
Bridgend
02920 705780

Menai Marine
Caernarfon
01286 677445

Relcal Marine
Tenby
01834 831714

Windjammer
Milford Haven
01646 699070

Marine Supplies
Gwent
01495 216309

New Quay Marine
New Quay
01545 561117

Rudders Boatyard
Burton
01646 600288

MES Marine
Queensferry
01244 289977

Cardigan O/Bs
Cardigan
01239 613966

West Point Marine
Cardiff
02920 373400

Ian Williams
Pwllheli
01758 720472

Lloyds Marine
Tenby
01646 686283

Yellowfin Marine
Cardiff
02920 373400

Kelpie Boats
Pembroke Dock
01646 683661

G G F Marine
Bridgend
01656 720498

Channel Islands
Mainbrayce
Alderney
01481 822772

OSR
Guernsey
01481 256839

Dave Warn Marine
St Helier
01534 853010

Iron Stores
St Helier
01534 850058

ISLE OF MAN
Halls Marine
Peel
01624 844386

MJS Marine
Ballasalla
01624 822920

NORTHERN IRELAND
MCA Boats
Newry
028302 62309

M G Stitt
Larne
02893 382278

North South Marine
Lisnaskea
02867 721720

R F Marine
Craigavon
07790 828095

Marine Engines
Co Down
07831 311412

JMB Marine
Co Down
028 91229527

EIRE
Killen Marine
Dublin
00353 12853908

O'Sullivans Marine
Tralee
00353 667124524

K. Duffy
Galway
00353 093 35449

Atlantic Boating
Skibbereen
00353 2822145

Palmerston Stores
Galway
00353 909741071

Cork Marine
Cork
00353 21 4845110

Yacht Agencies
Wicklow
00353 40432294

Motor Marine Co
Donegal
00353 749542277

ENGLAND
Outboard Services
Lostwithiel,
Cornwall
01208 873515

Birchell Marine
Torquay, Devon
01803 214305

Birchell Marine
Paignton, Devon
01803 558760

Wills Marine
Kingsbridge,
Devon
01548 852424

South Coast Marine
Christchurch,
Dorset
01202 482695

Poole Marine
Poole, Dorset
01201 677387

Oakley Motors
Brighton, E
Sussex
01273 603322

Walkers Chandlery
Leigh on Sea,
Essex
01702 421321

Fairweather Marine
Fareham, Hants
01329 283500

Powertech Marine
Hayling Island
0239 2637 222

Bembridge Motors
Bembridge, IOW
01983 873744

Chas Newens
Putney
0208 788 4587

Pro Rig Marine
Chertsey
01932 570202

Liverpool Boats
Bootle,
Merseyside
01519 441163

Beeston Marina
Beeston, Notts
01159 223 168

Lincoln Marine
East Bridgeford,
Notts
01949 21122

Race & Marine
Taunton,
Somerset
01823 282662

Seamark Nunn
Felixstowe,
Suffolk
01394 451000

Powerhouse Marine
Blaydon, Tyne/
Wear
01914 140065

Meridian Marine
Sutton Coldfield,
W Mids
0121 323 2333

SCOTLAND
Mitchell Outboards
Renfrew
01418 864222

DDZ Marine
Largs
01475 686072

Bosun's Locker
South
Queensferry
01313 314496

WALES
Dulas Boats
Dulas
01248 410266

Gower Marine
Burry Port
01792 390602

Llyn Marine
Glan-Y-Don
01758 612606

Quinquari Marine
St Davids
01437 721911

IRELAND
Newmills Marine
Coleraine
02870 343535

Duffy & Son
Co. Galway
035 39335449

Viking Marine
Co. Wicklow
0353 12811168

Marine Motors
Co. Cork
0353 214354217